CHRISTIANITY: A HISTORICAL RELIGION?

CHRISTIANITY:
A HISTORICAL RELIGION?

by
WILLIAM WAND

*Former Archbishop of Brisbane
and Bishop of London*

JUDSON PRESS
VALLEY FORGE PENNSYLVANIA

ISBN 0-8170-0554-4
Library of Congress Catalog Card No. 77-180505
Judson Press Edition 1972
Printed in Great Britain

Preface

The field of combat between faith and unfaith is for ever shifting. During the nineteenth century the struggle lay between science and religion. A satisfactory conclusion was not reached until both sides had agreed that each had a large territory of its own with its own especial methods and attitudes into which the other had no desire to force an entry: the no-man's-land between them could be left to common exploration.

In the twentieth century the battleground has moved from science to history, the reason being chiefly due to changes in the philosophy of history. The traditional conception of the nature of history has been subjected to very careful analysis and criticism. It must be admitted that the professional historians have not been so moved by these inquiries as have the philosophers. While the historians as a body still claim that it is possible by careful research to arrive at the precise truth of past events, the philosophers are inclined to the belief that every record of the past is so coloured by contemporary (and later) attitudes that precise exactitude is impossible.

This is to state the situation in a ridiculously inadequate fashion, but it is as well at least to glance at an extreme view in order to realise from the outset the nature of the problem at issue. It becomes clear at once that, if the question is of

5

importance to the secular historian, it must be even more fundamental to the theologian. The questions with which the secular historian deals may be of importance for the future regulation of our lives in time, but those with which the theologian deals are of importance for eternity. If therefore the latter teaches that his faith is grounded in history, it becomes of paramount importance for him to make sure that his history is securely founded. If the philosophers tell him that it is virtually impossible to have certain knowledge of anything in the past, he must obviously be concerned to find out whether their assertion can be seriously maintained.

Hence the flood of writing on the subject since the first decade of the twentieth century. So far the discussion has been carried on mostly among the professionals. No doubt it will soon penetrate to the man in the street and in the pew. It is well then that we should try to put into popular form what is already common to the experts. It will at least give the amateur a chance of knowing what the discussion is all about, and may even, if he is a man of faith, give him an opportunity of strengthening his belief against growing misapprehension.

He may even be induced to join with the *avant-garde* in an endeavour to find some other basis for his faith than disputed facts in the past. If history no longer appears a sure foundation, is it worth while to explore the possibilities of myth or of symbol? Both of them have been much canvassed in recent years. It is not implied that either can possess the utter reliability that was once attributed to history. But at least, it is said, they provide pointers; and it is suggested that an accumulation of such directives may furnish as good authority for belief as history itself.

But there still remain many, perhaps a majority, who feel that if historical fact disappears, Christianity will have lost its prop and stay. Jesus will have gone and with him the main reason for believing in God, eternity and the human soul.

It would therefore seem of paramount importance that we should find an answer to the question posed in the title of this book.

Contents

Introduction

Definition of Terms

Is Christianity a historical religion? It all depends, of course, on what we mean by history and by religion. Both terms have been much tortured of late and we shall presently have to examine their precise connotation with some care. But without going into technical details about either term for the moment there is some room for difference of opinion about the general application of the phrase as a whole.

What do we mean by a 'historical religion'? Well, we do not mean what an Australian means when he says that he finds Europe fascinating because it is 'such a historical kind of place'. He is evidently thinking of all the architectural reminders of a bygone age, which are perhaps all the more fascinating to him if they have no further use in the present than to provide objectives for the tourist traffic.

The great Christian feasts like Christmas, Easter, Ascension, Whitsuntide, profess to be commemorations of historic events. But they are not at all like the secular historic celebrations of Guy Fawkes Day, Trafalgar Day or even Armistice Day. The latter are commemorations of past events which may in due time be emptied of all present significance. Already the question is raised in many quarters whether it is worthwhile carrying on with Armistice Day at all, and whether, if we do carry on with it, we should not deliberately alter the balance of meaning and sentiment it has held for us so far and make it more 'up to date'.

The great Christian feasts are not like that at all. No one would dream of changing their significance. The historic events they commemorate have not been left behind on a half-forgotten page of history: they permanently endure. The acts of God are eternal. The particular event in time is an expression of an indelible element in the eternal character of God.

The Christian celebrations are, to use a pregnant expression, liturgical memorials. He who takes part in them remembers a past event, of course, but it is an event whose action still survives and in which the celebrant is actually caught up. Jesus is always being born into this sphere of time and space; he is still crucified, and the Christ is still risen, ascended, glorified. The believer, who is made one with him, is said by St. Paul to re-live these experiences in his own person.[1] Christianity is not just a piece of bygone chronology: it is incorporation into the living Christ.

The recollection of this fundamental fact should help us to be clear about what we mean when we call Christianity a historical religion. That there were datable events at the origins of the Christian faith is accepted by everyone who is not just a crank, although the number of them and the degree to which they are necessary to the faith is now hotly disputed. But the important thing is that, according to the Catholic Religion, they are not over and done with: they still survive both in their effects and as expressions of ever-present truth, which becomes part and parcel, not only of the believer's intellectual equipment, but of his very life.

To say, then, that Christianity is a historical religion means more than that it is associated with events in the past. It implies that the past events with which it is associated have an essential importance in the present. It suggests that the history still lives, and that it is somehow bound up together with the salvation of the world and of the individual both here and hereafter.

Looking at the subject in this way, we realise how important to Christianity the past actually is. Obviously, if we are even approximately correct so far, we cannot dispense with it altogether. We cannot regard the Christian challenge as something that comes to us out of the blue without any background in past events.

But, we are entitled to ask, does this apply to all the alleged events in Christianity's past or only to some of them? Are the less critical or important events easily expendable while the few outstanding ones demand retention at whatever cost? If we cling to the empty tomb must we also assert the raising of Lazarus? If we deny the Annunciation can we still affirm the Incarnation?

Obviously if we agree that some alleged facts may be allowed to disappear while others for safety's sake must be retained, we shall have to decide how and where the line is to be drawn. It would be at least interesting to know whether there are any general principles that can decide the answer or whether every case must be taken on its merits.

He would be an odd person who did not regard such questions as both interesting and important. In any case they are the questions with which we shall be concerned in this book. We begin by reminding ourselves of the conventional answer that is still given by the people whom most of us perhaps consider old-fashioned. We then consider the kind of answer that is more likely to be given today. After that we can follow the argument where it leads.

Notes

1 Rom. 6: 3 ff.

1

The Conventional Answer

1 History

We begin then by reminding ourselves what is the solution commonly offered. The man in the street or in the pew would almost certainly reply as a matter of course that Christianity is strictly a historical religion. If he were asked to give a reason, he would probably without any hesitation say 'The Bible'. He would take it for granted that the Bible is a history book and that it contains the records of the origins both of Christianity itself and of the Judaism out of which it grew. A formidable array of documentary evidence indeed.

It will be admitted that there is something immensely attractive about this judgment, as there is about most plain and simple statements. We may even find later on that there is something to be said in support of it. But it must be confessed that from the outset some serious objections leap to the eye.

The first and most striking is that so far from Christianity being built upon historical documents, it actually preceded the collection we know as the New Testament. Christians of all kinds have developed so strong a mystique about the Bible that they sometimes mistake the true place of the scriptures in the development of Christianity. It is not always remembered, for instance, that the only Bible the primitive Church had was what we know as the Old Testament and that the New Testament did not take its final shape until well into the fourth century. The first person who promulgated precisely the same list of books as is contained in our canon was St. Athanasius in A.D. 346; and it was still a couple of centuries or so before that list was pronounced authoritative for the universal Church.

Of course Christians were using these books from the time they were written (Paul, the earliest of our accepted writers, began his letters in or about A.D. 50), but the point is that it was long after the Church's history was well under way before there was an accepted collection of literary material which could be regarded as the foundation documents of the Christian faith.

It must be admitted, however, in some slight mitigation of this judgment that, through its inclination to interpret prophecy as history before the event, the early Church felt that it had a reliable historical source for its own life and work in the Old Testament (the Jewish Bible). But at least the New Testament was never the foundation document of the Church in the same sense as that in which a testator's will is the foundation for a charity or an Act of Parliament the basis for a law.

Another easy objection to the popular view of Christianity as a historical religion based on the Bible is that it exaggerates the Bible's own claim to be a collection of historical documents. Actually the Bible is an anthology of many kinds of writing culled from a national literature covering about twelve hundred years. It is obvious that from the purely historical point of view such varied types of writing must have very different values. Poetry, laws, ethics, mythology, visions, novels, sermons must have unequal uses from the point of view of the historian. The old method of reading the Bible as if it were all meant to be taken in the same literal spirit of dry-as-dust history is to pay insufficient heed to the individual genius of the respective writers and has been almost universally abandoned.

We still, however, have to go some distance before we have properly recognised the differing quality of writers who might be classed together as generally historical. Compare for instance the respective aims of the authors of the third and fourth gospels. Here is St. Luke, "It seemed good to me, having traced the course of all things accurately from the first, to write a connected narrative for you, so that you may know the certainty of the matters wherein you have been instructed" (1:3). And here is St. John, "These things are written that you may believe that Jesus is the Christ, the Son of God, and that believing you may have life in his name" (20:31).

It would be difficult to imagine a sharper contrast. The one says, in effect, "I am going to write a piece of precise and accurate history": the other says, "I have written a piece of frank propaganda." St. Luke comes as near, in intention at least, as any ancient writer, to what we should call scientific history. Whether he succeeded in fulfilling his intention is of course another matter, and one about which the most diverse opinions are held at the present time.

The author of the fourth gospel makes no such claim. He says candidly that he has been writing in order to persuade. Since he has so openly declared his intention, we cannot hold it against him that he writes from a special point of view. There is, in any case, nothing necessarily sinister about the term 'propaganda'. But one does not expect the same objective writing from the propagandist as from the historian. The latter emphasises what he believes to be facts, while the former emphasises the interpretation he wishes to put on them.

In practice it is not always easy to distinguish between the two roles and perhaps they always overlap. The propagandist must state what he takes to be facts before he begins to interpret them, and the historian would be a very dull dog if he merely stated what he took to be facts without telling us what they mean.

With this intriguing situation we shall have to deal at length later on. Meanwhile we may notice that in the opinion of many scholars the two writers whom we are quoting have changed roles, so that St. Luke is reckoned less of a historian and more of a propagandist than he thinks he is, while St. John's reputation as an objective historian has improved quite considerably in the current century.

To revert to our main topic of consideration in this chapter, it seems clear that both the long story of the formation and authorisation of the canon and the varied quality of the scriptural books prevent us from accepting quite simply the popular view that the Bible is a sufficient guarantee of Christianity as a historical religion. We shall have to do a good deal of thinking about the nature of history before we can make up our minds whether proper qualifications and modifications will enable us to accept the proposition in any sense at all.

2 Religion

The connotation of the term 'religion', as generally accepted, is very wide. Essentially it means a relation towards

God. This relation is usually taken to include at least three things: the mental attitude induced by the recognition of God or of some ruling, spiritual power; the moral attitude resulting from such a belief and dictating ethical conduct; and the credal statements and rites of worship in which the belief is expressed. In actual practice it is never easy to hold all three elements in equipoise, and the idea of religion changes its complexion according as the chief emphasis is placed on one element or another.

It is sometimes complained that the English temper finds the second element most agreeable to its own genius and is therefore inclined to think of religion as beginning and ending in morality. Those, on the other hand, who are prone to emphasise the third element often have a special grudge against those who stress the first, on the ground that by so doing they turn religion into a mere philosophy. Far the most frequent attacks, however, are made by those who favour the first. They turn the tables by saying that those who emphasise creeds and liturgies are apt to make religion into mere external observance, and thereby to lose its living heart and core.

It is this last objection which has made a rift in the use of the term 'religion' between the ordinary Christian and the theologians, or at least such of them as are most influenced by current German thought and are most ready to claim the authority of some of our own Reformation divines. It is not that the recognition of such a distinction between a religion of the heart and one of mere form is something new. It can be traced back to the beginning of Christianity and indeed into the Old Testament itself. The brazen serpent that was the means of salvation to the children of Israel in the

19

wilderness, became to later generations no more than Nehushtan—a piece of brass, an idolatrous obstruction to any heartfelt religion; and Hezekiah experienced no compunction in destroying it (2 Kings 18:4).

It might be claimed that the need to release true spiritual force from the fetters of systematisation was the real justification of the Reformation. But it would have to be remembered that new systems soon took the place of the old and that the 'confessions' of the reformed Churches were much more detailed, bulky, and confusing than the historic creeds of ancient Christendom.

No doubt the need to break the shell in order to get at the kernel is felt from time to time in all religion (as it was apparently by Akhenaton in the Egypt of the fourteenth century B.C.[1]). But as long as the kernel remains alive and growing it will need the protection, the incentive and the moulding influence of the shell.

It is therefore a pity that so many writers of the present generation have made the mistake of first identifying religion with what we have claimed to be its third component only, systematisation, whether of statement or of ceremony, and then denouncing it as if it meant, and could mean, no more than the dead hand of legalism preventing the free-flowing life of the spirit. The idiosyncrasies of personal temperament and fortune may excuse a Kierkegaard or Bonhoeffer for talking in such a fashion. But it is not so easy to excuse some of our own divines for taking a perfectly good, well-known term (whatever its etymology) and limiting it in this peculiar and partial way. One can well understand the perplexity of a congregation when they hear their pastor denouncing as evil an activity which they had always taken as the very reason for his professional existence.

In this book at least we shall try to adhere to the common and popular meaning of the word. When we ask whether Christianity is a historical religion, we mean by religion an attitude of reverence towards God, the moral commitment implied by such an attitude, and the forms of belief and worship in which it is expressed.

Notes

[1] Generally known as Amenophis IV (1372–1354 B.C.). Tried to introduce a new national religion centring in the worship of the sun (Aton).

2

The Current View of History

After this digression to consider the nature of religion we can return to our consideration of history, trying this time to get a little nearer to a more scientific and professional view than is represented by the popular notion we dealt with in earlier pages.

1 The Task of the Historian

And here let us say at once, that by history we do not mean merely a series of events in the past but the systematic record of such events. Some scholars would limit the record, if it is to be regarded as strictly historical, to those events which have a direct influence upon human beings. Thus an account of the happenings in the solar system before man appeared on the earth would not be history. On the other hand we have to remember the use of the word in the phrase 'Natural History', which in common usage excludes man. And we must also remember that some, if not all, events in the 'natural' order have a direct or indirect effect on human beings, and should therefore be duly dealt with in any adequate history of their period, as for instance the eruption of Mt. Vesuvius and the consequent destruction of Pompeii and its inhabitants on 24 August, A.D. 79.

The Current View of History

In general we can take it for granted that history is not much interested in events except in so far as they concern human beings. There is, however, another and much more serious limitation, which is not always remembered. History is concerned only with such events as happen within the space-time continuum. Events, real or imagined, which occur in an eternal or spiritual sphere are not the proper subject of history. The reason is that history has no tools by which it can deal with such events. In so far as it is scientific, history is a form of measurement. It can estimate the amount of evidence for or against a given event and can sometimes measure the credibility of the evidence. But the evidence is documentary, whether of stone, parchment or paper, including evidence of an archaeological nature; and none of these belongs to the intangible sphere of spirit.

The historian does indeed come in contact with alleged spiritual events but only at the point where they show their effect within the human world. He does not feel himself entitled to pass judgment on the Angels of Mons, except in so far as he might record any access of courage that belief in their appearance may have afforded to the troops. Or, to take a biblical instance, the historian may very well be asked to give his view of the evidence for the empty tomb, while being told at the same time that he is in no privileged position as a historian to express a view on the resurrection of Jesus. This latter illustration is all the more telling because some theologians appear loath to distinguish between one event and the other, between the empty tomb and the resurrection, but let their dislike of the idea of a 'physical' resurrection spill over into a rejection of the story of the empty tomb. We shall have to deal with this point later.

23

If now we limit history to what happens to human beings and to what happens within the sphere of space and time, can we go on to give a more positive description of it?

It is commonly believed that the subject-matter of history is irrefutable fact and only irrefutable fact. It is the business of the historian to discover the ascertainable facts and then to set them down. So long did history enjoy the reputation of being an established collection of concrete events that it was exalted in both learned and popular esteem as the supreme judge among the arts and sciences. Everything must be brought before the bar of history for its final verification. Whatever could not pass the test of historical inquiry must be classed as legend or myth: only history could claim an invariable access to reality.

The still waters of this fixed habit of thought were disturbed in this country when R. G. Collingwood began to popularise in Oxford the ideas of the Italian professor Benedetto Croce. Collingwood's *Idea of History* was published in 1946 but he had been lecturing on the subject at least ten years before that. Croce had written his great book *La Storia* in 1912–13, but the translation *History as the Story of Liberty* was not published in English until 1941. Since then there has been a continual stream of books and articles exploring the field of discussion and endeavouring, without much success so far, to reach definitive conclusions.

We can at least go some way towards defining the problem. The difficulty lies in the fact that, as we have seen, it has generally been taken for granted that history deals solely with facts. The record, as it was written, approximated as closely as possible to events as they happened. History, in this sense, was the minute-book of past ages, recording only the business done. Written out strictly from this point of view it would be little more than a chronicle, the setting of a date and time to each event of the past.

In point of fact, however, no one ever does write history like that. There must always be an attempt to afford some perspective, to distinguish between the important and the unimportant, to trace the course of cause and effect. Added to which there is always the need to describe the personalities in the great drama, to explain the influence of character upon the action as it proceeds. History is not history without the human story.

It is partly upon this point that the famous controversy turns as to whether history is to be regarded as a branch of science or as a branch of art. Is it a research report or is it literature? The fact that some of our finest examples of English prose have been written as histories must not be allowed to disguise from us the fact that most contemporary historians regard their essential business as that of inquiring into events. Whether their setting forth of the facts they discover results in literature is largely a matter of indifference. The point with which we are dealing is not, however, just a question of the charm of fine writing. The real division is between those who think that history is essentially a plain statement of fact and those who think that it is much more, not only in the matter of style but also of content.

Today no philosopher-historian has any doubt that the latter is the correct view. However determined a historian may be to commit to paper a plain, objective, impartial account of the past, he simply cannot do so. To begin with, he cannot crowd all the events of his period into his manuscript: he must make a selection. But in making the selection his own personality is bound to reveal itself. He will be guided by his own views as to what is important and what is not. It is like the difference between a painting and a photograph. In every painting the personality of the artist is seen as much in what he has left out of his canvas as in what he has inserted.

But the difference goes much further than mere selection. There is of necessity also an element of interpretation. Even in the plainest statement of an event or a set of circumstances it is impossible to eliminate the point of view of the beholder. It is well known in the criminal courts that no two honest witnesses will agree precisely in their account of the same event. Even when they least suspect it, they are interpreting what they have seen.

How much more inevitable must be this unsuspected interpretation in the case of the historian dealing with vast, complicated and often hotly controverted movements. Pure objectivity remains impossible. In the course of years the writer has developed his own view, or else he has been conditioned by his environment to accept a view developed in the national or group interest. If the extent of this consistent 'brain-washing' were doubted, one might reflect on the change that would be effected in two nations if, for instance, American and English schoolboys were to exchange history books for a generation.

So far is the writing of history affected by the influence of contemporary thought that some philosophers have contended that, even apart from the judgments consciously and deliberately passed by the historian, all written history reflects more of current thought than of the age with which it deals. In fact Croce went so far as to coin the aphorism "All history is contemporary philosophy."

Whatever may be our judgment on this issue, it is clear that in the sphere of history we can no longer walk with as firm a step as did our fathers. We have been forced to recognise more clearly than they did how much every record is coloured by such influences as selection, characterisation and interpretation. The question therefore arises: what attitude towards the records of the past ought we to adopt?

2 Our Attitude Towards It

Everyone knows in practical life how important is the initial attitude of mind with which one approaches any question. In the army every man, whether officer or other ranks, who fears that he may be the possible object of an inquiry, is anxious to get his report in first. In civil life the lawyer's clients know that his emotional approach to a case is nearly as important as his knowledge of the law. In the social circle our hostess is always anxious that we should get a good first impression of her other guests, and so primes us carefully before we meet them. In respect of our attitude to the world in general, it makes a lot of difference whether we are disapproving, dubious, or receptive.

Whoever we are, and whatever we do, the temperament of approach is fundamentally important. It may be possible in physical experiments to create a balance in a vacuum, but one cannot achieve that unbiassed equity in the sphere of thought. Consciously or unconsciously, everyone chooses whether he will adopt an affirmative, a hesitant, or a negative *weltanschauung*. Anyone who thinks he has a good working knowledge of his own character may take precautions against excess in any one direction, but it can never be easy to change essentially one's natural disposition, although we may try to recognise our own particular idiosyncrasy and so to guard against its influence on our judgment.

More than three centuries ago the dubious attitude was deliberately adopted by Descartes. As is well known, he resolved to doubt everything, even his own existence, until he found a satisfactory proof of it. Some thinkers believe that with the imitation of Descartes the whole of European philosophy took a wrong turn. Whether that be true or not, it is safe to say that in this respect all Western philosophy has ever since been profoundly influenced by Descartes' emphasis on the need to reckon with doubt.

Today that doubting spirit has entered the sphere of history with particular force. There its influence could be much more devastating than, for instance, in the sphere of physics, where a doubt may soon be resolved by actual experiment. In history to entertain a doubt is often in effect to give a negative decision, because what is doubtful must be eliminated from the whole field of cause and effect.

Such a risk should be kept in mind by those historians who consider that every fact must be doubted until it is proved. One is reminded of the allegedly French axiom that every defendant is guilty until his innocence is demonstrated. This attitude is generally contrasted with the English principle that every man is innocent until he is proved guilty. It is not merely patriotism that makes one prefer the latter as a working rule. It is probably a more satisfactory manner of approach in thought as well as in life. Of course, from whichever principle you start, everything must in the end be subject to examination, and one must endeavour to eliminate prejudice and temperament in order to be as unbiassed as possible in coming to a conclusion. But one's initial attitude remains important, not least if one makes exaggerated efforts to guard against it.

It makes a great deal of difference whether one is ready to give any weight to authority. Obviously, when we are children, we have to live by authority. In the preparatory school the boys are ready to accept any dictum of their master. (This remains true in spite of modern methods of co-operative study.) But later, when they are working their way towards the sixth form, they are gradually weaned from this reliance on the teacher. By the time they reach the university they are taught to test every authority in proportion to their own capacity for research.

Such a process, however desirable, can never be perfect. No man can ever discover everything for himself, and if he lives in an atmosphere of perpetual doubt, he becomes a menace to himself and to everyone else. He is fortunate if, in the matters that are most important to him, he can acquire enough knowledge and expertise to test other men's assertions for himself, while still being able to rest the remainder of his design for living upon authorities he can trust. All of us, however academically expert, must continue to live 'between the lights', in a twilight world where illumination is compounded part of self-reliance and part of outside support.

It would seem then that the right attitude to adopt in historical matters is neither that of total doubt nor of total credulity, but of caution. In particular where history impinges on the sphere of religion, we shall not be over-disposed to accept a supernatural explanation just because it is supernatural, nor to reject it just because we dislike the supernatural anyway. As we have already suggested, it is no part of the historian's task to prove or to disprove the supernatural. He is concerned only with alleged causes or effects within time and space. And with regard to those he must be as openminded as he can. If physical causation does not seem sufficient to explain the phenomena with which he has to deal, he will not regard a 'supernatural' cause as impossible. Even where there are possible 'natural' alternatives, he will be prepared to accept the supernatural, if it seems to offer the better explanation of the circumstances as a whole.

Thus, for instance, if our inquirer is dealing with the period of Old Testament history, he will certainly, as historian, have to begin where any secular historian would, describing the tribal origins of the Jewish people, tracing their course among the movements of surrounding nations, and estimating the influence of their human and natural environment on their religion and culture. But in reading the Old Testament itself he will come across an entirely different type of explanation for the peculiar character of the Jewish people. They were chosen, we are told, for their particular destiny by God himself, who revealed his own nature to them, took them for his particular allies, and used them as means by which he could reveal himself to the world. Our inquirer will have to ask whether these two descriptions of the course of history are mutually exclusive or whether they can be seen somehow to dovetail into one another and so prove mutually supporting.

If this kind of problem faces him in regard to the whole course of Old Testament history, it will show itself with poignancy in respect of many separate events in that history.

Take for instance the crossing of the Red (or Reed) Sea. Granted that the event, or something like it, actually took place, was the flood that drowned the Egyptians a purely natural phenomenon, or did 'God speak and it was done'? If the inquirer feels that the subsequent history is best explained by the belief that God 'overwhelmed his enemies in the Red Sea', then he must surely leave room for the possibility that the belief was, and is, well-founded.

Into the psychological question whether the belief could have had the same effect, so long as it was held, even if it had not been correct, it is no part of our present business at the moment to enter. We hope we have said enough to show the importance of an open mind in all historical inquiry and particularly where the concern is with religious history. As we shall see later, it is impossible to come to the consideration of such questions without some kind of bias. The right attitude is, as far as possible, to recognise the bias and to be prepared to allow for it.

3

Knowledge and Faith

It may be well, before we go any further in this essay, again to digress a little in order to inquire what we mean by 'knowledge' and how we can delimit its sphere.

In the present state of public opinion the scientist gains a good deal of credit because it is generally supposed that he, in distinction from other scholars, proceeds only upon a basis of certain knowledge. Perhaps that is why so many historians are anxious to have their special technique included among the sciences, so that they may share the support popularly given to their scientific colleagues. It is obvious, however, that history cannot be numbered among those sciences whose claims can be justified by experiments. If, therefore, the historian can make good his claim to knowledge, it will not be to the same kind of knowledge as is asserted in the case of his scientific colleague.

It is popularly supposed that the theologian also lays claim to knowledge, a knowledge that comes not from discovery but from revelation. And that, no doubt, is why he is so often asked to give proof of his claims. It is expected that he will provide logical demonstrations of the same order as the mathematicians' demonstration that two and two make four, a demonstration that leaves no room for doubt in the mind of any sane person. But this is to misunderstand the status of theology. It occasionally gives rise to some derision when it is found that the theologian is not claiming ability to furnish this kind of proof or knowledge at all, but relies on something he calls faith; it is gratuitously assumed that he substitutes faith for reason. Does this mean that there are different kinds of knowledge, differently apprehended?

We may take it that to 'know' a thing is to be completely certain about it, with a certainty that leaves no room for doubt. It is sometimes said that in this sense there are only two kinds of knowledge, mathematical conclusions and physical sensations. Actually both have been submitted to question. Mathematicians point out that their certainty rests ultimately upon faith in the stability of the universe, namely that the rule 'two and two make four' will remain as valid tomorrow as it is today—a belief which the theory of relativity seemed at one time likely to call in question. As for physical contact, anyone who suffers from a simple attack of migraine will know that, when the period of numbness sets in, the touching of a material object may bring no sensation at all.

Apart, however, from these refinements, we all generally accept it as a fact that there is an area of awareness that can be properly called knowledge, a certainty that admits of no doubt in the mind of the thinker. With this state of mind faith, as properly conceived, is sharply contrasted. If knowledge admits no possibility of doubt, faith cannot exist without the possibility of doubt. Faith is a moral as well as an intellectual faculty: it is exercised by the will as well as by the intellect. It implies not only awareness but also acceptance and trust. It must overcome the obstacle of doubt; and that it cannot normally do without an element of goodwill, a readiness to be convinced.

Faith thus includes both 'belief that' and 'belief in'. You must believe that an event happened before you can accept it as having any importance for you: you must believe that a person exists before you can put any trust in him. That is why it is a mistake to think that faith can do without reason. In the 'believing that' stage faith has to employ precisely the same ratiocination as knowledge. The only difference is that it cannot go so far: it cannot reach the absolute certainty that is knowledge. A gap remains; and that is filled by the 'belief in', that is, by the leap over the void to the side of the person or object contemplated. Such faith involves the determination to risk the effort, the expenditure of energy, required by the need to serve the interests of that in which we believe. It is thus seen that faith, although less conclusive, is a far more complicated and moral affair than mere knowledge.

One result of this greater effort on the part of faith is to make it much more personal and intimate than knowledge. It may therefore assume a greater importance, and even, paradoxical as it may seem, practical certainty. One's faith in a trusted leader may seem much more real and vital than one's knowledge of the date of Waterloo. Because of this added importance writers, particularly the sacred writers, often speak of faith as if it were knowledge. St. Paul actually contrasts knowledge in the sense of physical awareness with knowledge exclusively of a spiritual and moral type, much to the advantage of the latter: he can speak of 'walking by faith' rather than by sight; (cf. 2 Cor. 5:7), also 2 Cor. 5:16: "From now on I no longer recognise people by their physical

34

attributes. Even if I had known Christ in the flesh, I should know him in that way no longer."

The fourth gospel continually talks of 'knowing' God. This complicates the issue for us, but the problem is eased if it is realised that 'knowledge' is here used in the sense of understanding God, of entering into the mystery of the divine character.

The examination of the relation between knowledge and faith is important for our present consideration, because it must be clear on reflection that the Bible aims at producing the second rather than the first kind of knowledge—that which comes by faith not sight. This does not mean that the two are in conflict, but that the biblical writers are less interested in handing on information than in producing an attitude of mind. They want above all things to influence men's relation towards God and his purposes. This statement applies to the writers both of the Old Testament and of the New. The former are anxious that succeeding generations of their people shall know what mercies God has shown to his chosen race. The latter are anxious that the leading facts in the earthly life of the Saviour of mankind shall be universally understood as revealing the character of God. Both are more interested in their readers' reaction to the facts than in their mere knowledge of them. In this respect Moses' injunction to teach the young the meaning of the Passover is of the same order as the fourth gospel's ready assertion "These things are written that ye may believe" (Exod. 13:8, 9; John 20:31).

To distinguish between faith and knowledge is not therefore to suggest that faith can reach no measure of certainty at all. Just because faith involves more of the personality,

35

requiring an effort of the will as well as of the intellect, it can be held with greater effective conviction than mere knowledge. Indeed faith, to be true, must always include preparedness to act upon the belief, whereas knowledge requires no such corollary at all. The well-known Socratic aphorism, 'Knowledge is virtue', was only possible because knowledge was interpreted, not in the purely scientific sense common today, but with the implied addition of a practical readiness to act, such as we ascribe to faith. It may indeed be said that faith leads to an improved kind of knowledge, since, if you have faith in a person, you are in the best position to understand him and so to know him. But these niceties tend to obscure the main issue, and for our purpose it is best to keep the concepts of faith and knowledge separate. That will serve us best when we come to deal with the problems of history and belief.

But one point does emerge which we must be prepared to face honestly. Since the term knowledge was not defined in ancient times as carefully as it is today, it is likely that writers of an early period would be less careful about accepting items of information as authoritative knowledge than would a responsible author of our generation. Stories of the supernatural, statements about miracles, memories of natural portents would be more easily accepted then than now. People lived in a different conceptual atmosphere from that which is characteristic of our own times.

Such a mental tendency would help to blur the sharp distinction between what was known and what was only believed. From the opposite side also the barrier would be eroded. The fact is that belief was often much more firmly held than it is among ourselves. The men of genius who led the early Christian movement, such as Paul and John, lived in a largely hostile environment and went in constant fear of their lives. They were hardly likely to do that for a mere hypothesis or vague possibility. They had to believe intensely what they were prepared to risk so much for, and that very intensity made faith seem much like knowledge. There is in any case a sense in which one may grasp with greater practical effectiveness a reality that is believed in by faith than one that is held by rational knowledge. The barrier between the two appears completely down in the kind of language that speaks of 'knowing God by faith',[1] but even in such a phrase there is an implied assumption that there will be a still more concrete and certain kind of knowledge when we have the privilege of knowing God by sight.

This discussion seemed advisable in order that we might remind ourselves that religious and historical 'knowledge' may not be so far asunder as is often assumed. In spite of Newman we do not have to call upon any special 'illative' sense in order to justify religious knowledge. While it is true that one cannot 'prove' religious statements by the methods and to the extent still available to 'prove' historical events, it is also true that the same general sense of the credible and the same general ratiocination are, or can be, employed in both cases. Indeed it might be said with justice that a religious affirmation has the advantage in this respect because it is made with a larger element of the total personality.

Notes

[1] Collect for Epiphany.

4

Legend, Myth and Symbol

In recent years, while the more careful exploration of the meaning of history has been going on, it has become obvious that there are a number of literary genres that hover on the outskirts between history and fiction without belonging exactly to either. Of those the three most important are legend, myth and symbol. They all belong in greater or less degree to the region of para-history, of *ersatz* history, of substitute history. The recent discussions have brought them all into prominence. If history itself has seemed to fail us, may we not get some comfort from one of these less exacting ways of considering the past? Conversely, if any one of these adumbrations of history can tell us so much, ought we not to be more nearly satisfied than we are with the much more that we can get from reputed history itself? In any case all three genres have acquired a new respectability from their recognised approximation to the picture of history. Consequently they each deserve separate examination.

1

Perhaps the simplest of the three terms is legend. It means by derivation 'something to be read', and was applied originally to the stories of the saints which were regularly read during communal meals in monastic assemblies. The point of the reading was to inspire devotion: there was in the material read very little effort at historical accuracy; although there was generally some substratum of truth, or the readings would hardly have been credible even in an uncritical age.

Inevitably the proportion of truth to fiction varied with each legend. Some had a very large percentage of actual fact while others had scarcely any. Consequently the name of 'legend' did not rank very high with those who began to feel some yearning for literal accuracy. Among the nineteenth-century positivist historians the designation 'mere legend' was enough to condemn a story at once as of no account. The result was that much valuable material was thrown into the discard.

Today legend has made something of a recovery in scholarly esteem. Largely owing to the discoveries of the archaeologists, it has been shown that the background of many legends does actually belong to the precise period of which they portend to treat. Although this revelation cannot of itself prove the correctness of the narrative concerned, it does at least lend it a certain air of verisimilitude. It is now generally conceded that such narratives may indeed add something of real value to our general knowledge of the period. Above all, the life stories of great heroes, with which the legends deal, are now taken with much more seriousness than in the recent past. Thus, for instance, classical students are more ready to accept Homer as a single author than once they were, and to divine some actual reality behind his stories of the journeys and wars of his heroes. Similarly Old Testament scholars are prepared to see rather more genuine history

39

in the biographies of the Patriarchs and Moses than they once were.

2

If the admixture of fact and fancy in a legend was originally treated as a matter of some indifference, the myth was regarded, until recently, by scientific historians as all false. A myth was 'a *purely fictitious* narrative involving supernatural persons or natural phenomena'.[1] It generally concerned pagan gods or goddesses, who in any case had no existence, or else it embodied the processes of nature in a tale. Indeed the term 'myth' not only suggested fiction but was commonly used as plainly asserting total lack of substantial fact. To say that something was 'myth' was precisely to affirm that it had no historical value whatever.

That is still the common usage of the term. Unfortunately in technical use it has come to bear a different and almost contradictory sense. It is now taken to imply truth of a sort. This change is due to a slavish and quite unnecessary following of German practice, in which the term is applied to any considerable picture of the past without pausing in the first instance to ask whether it is fact or fiction. The truth it offers may be that of art or poetry, of morals or religion. It may even include some historic fact; but the term is applied indiscriminately to the whole story that has sprung up around some great alleged event or figure, whether fact or fable. Thus we may speak without prejudice of the 'myth' of creation, of the 'myth' of Napoleon. It has its counterpart in the current term 'image' as applied to the popular picture of some present-day notability, which the press or the political

40

party are supposed to build up in order to create a desired impression for the benefit of the general public. How far it has any connection with reality may be a question for debate.

It is a thousand pities that English theologians used so ambiguous and unscientific a term as a precision tool in their own language. They made their task of communication with the man in the pew much more difficult than it need have been. If they had used some other form of the word not already in common use, such for instance as *mythos*,[2] the public would then have been aware that they were being called upon to encounter what was to them a comparatively new conception. As it was, they were brought up short by hearing the New Testament stories of early Christianity, and even of Jesus himself, freely described as 'myth', the very term that the dictionaries explained as connoting fiction. It was natural that to many this should seem incomprehensible and to others plain blasphemy. From the resultant confusion we have not yet completely extricated ourselves.

It is believed by anthropologists that many of the most ancient myths spring from deep-lying psychological causes. They may well represent a folklore which itself embodies much primitive knowledge. The careful study of primitive myths can reveal a good deal about the universal beliefs and aspirations of mankind. They may disclose to the scientific investigator valuable information of a prehistorical order. Even the scientific historian can therefore not afford to ignore them.

One can realise all the more clearly how difficult and how important the investigation of myth becomes when we enter the historical period. How far do the same psychological impulses exercise a measurable influence? Will the same causes operate in developing the image of the 'wisest fool in Christendom' as did in creating that of the 'sweet psalmist of Israel'? And if so, will the intervening centuries have persuaded the myth-makers to work with greater accuracy? In any case, it is certainly true that one may see a myth growing before one's very eyes around a personage whom oneself has known. It may be fairly easy here and now to distinguish between the truth and the falsehood, but it will be much more difficult in a generation to come, when the stories can no longer be checked from personal knowledge. After all that has been written, who can be quite sure about the image of Winston Churchill?

All this should be sufficient to encourage us to exercise caution in dealing with records of the past. Certainly we must be careful to inquire what, if any, mythical elements have crept into the account. But we shall also be careful not to reject as worthless so-called myths, or to allow the name to be attached without explanation to records which may have some claim to historical valuation.

There is a special kind of myth which deals with the origin and rise of nations. Its purpose is to exalt the people whom it concerns, to give them a good conceit of themselves and to spur them to renewed efforts. It therefore glamorises the great figures of the old days and makes them appear the representatives of a specially chosen and favoured race. It may on occasion render the same service for a party or school of thought within the nation. "Such myths," says Alan Richardson, "are ideological interpretations of history. . . . It is not necessary that the myth should be true, but only that it should be 'useful'. Though ostensibly it interprets the past, its real concern is the future. . . . Myth is essentially 'practical history'."[3] To it successive writers, whether it be the Jewish Chronicler or the British Macaulay, make each his own contribution.

3

In many respects the most interesting of our three terms is the word 'symbol'. It has become extremely important in modern thought, especially in connection with the subject that is the theme of this book. Before we have finished we shall probably have to deal with it at some length. But already it is worth while considering it, if only in summary fashion: a proper understanding of it will greatly assist our subsequent discussion.

By derivation the word means something 'thrown together'. It suggested more than one level of significance and was applied to a distinctive mark, a token, an admission ticket. It was then used for a watchword, a slogan, a maxim, a creed. It is indeed the common word for a creed in early Christian writers, implying a brief form of words pointing to ineffable mysteries. It is thus regularly used for an indicator that suggests something beyond itself. It is a pointer that brings to mind some number, object, process, or person.

Like the term 'sign' in dogmatic theology 'symbol' is capable of a double use. A sign may be merely pictorial, pointing to something entirely outside itself, or it may be effective, actually conveying what it signifies. A flag may be the sign of the presence of some royal personage or other dignitary: an electric wire is the sign of an energy that it

43

actually conveys. So a symbol may point to a reality of which it forms itself no actual part, or it may itself be part of the actuality it represents. The ascension of Jesus is for some people no more than a vivid pictorial representation of Christ's triumph over evil, while for others it is both that and also the historical event by which the series of his appearances on earth was terminated. Thus a symbol may be a factual truth conveying a further and deeper meaning, or it may be a mere fiction conveying the same meaning (as we quite illogically say) 'realistically', that is, in a vivid and concrete picture.

If the symbol is put into narrative form, it may easily become a parable. Everyone knows the schoolboy's definition of a parable as 'an earthly story with a heavenly meaning', which has the naïve simplicity of genius. If we take the parables of Jesus as the standard, we recognise that, while none of them claims to be a true story, they are generally taken from common life and are consequently true in general if not in particular. And it is their general truth that forms the point of comparison with some spiritual reality. Probably no sower ever had on any one occasion the precise series of experiences recounted in the parable, but any sower *might* have had them in whole or in part; and it is the general fortune attendant upon the task of sowing that quite fittingly and legitimately gives rise to the spiritual comparison.

Today the symbolic method of writing has become of immense importance not only in poetry, where it has always been common, but also in novels and drama. Comparatively few people are prepared nowadays to accept a good story in and for itself as adequate entertainment. Everyone looks for a hidden meaning. In the drama, of course, the particular is expected to point to the universal. Few playwrights would be content if their plot could not be read on at least two different levels. T. S. Eliot went much further. When told that the members of a whole family of playgoers returning from *The Cocktail Party* had each interpreted the play differently, he replied, "But that is precisely what they are intended to do."

In such instances the distinction between fact and fiction does not seem to make any difference to the value of the artistic, moral, or religious truth conveyed. It is plain, however, that such a state of things must raise great issues when transferred to the sphere of history. Does it make the factual element in history less important?

One would be inclined to ask, if the psychological effect was the same, what could it matter whether the alleged facts were truth or invention? One would imagine, for instance, that Buddhism would remain much the same religion, even if the Buddha himself were proved to be a historical fiction. On the other hand there are some religions, or elements in a religion, which are so closely identified with historical reality that they would fade into non-existence altogether if it could be proved that they had no basis in historic fact. It is very unlikely, for instance, that Christianity could continue to exist, at any rate in its present form, if it were proved that Jesus never lived or that there had never been any incarnation.

It seems evident then that while we accept the symbolic as a worthy element in historical religion, we must be on our guard to preserve some place for historical reality within the symbolism itself. Some, at least, of the symbols must be in the technical sense 'effective' and not merely pictorial.

Christianity: A Historical Religion?

Notes

[1] Cf. Shorter Oxford English Dictionary, 2nd edition, 1936, Vol. 1.

[2] The President of St. Catherine's, Cambridge, follows Jung in suggesting *mythologem*. T. R. Henn, *Bible as Literature* (Lutterworth Press, 1970), p. 19.

[3] *History Sacred and Profane* (S.C.M., 1964), p. 245.

5

The Present Situation

At the moment Christians seem to be falling rapidly into two
contrasted sections, those who accept the allegedly historical
basis of their religion as, generally speaking, factual and those
who accept it only as symbolical. This division is no doubt
blurred at the edges, but it still strikes right across the
hitherto accepted barriers between parties and denominations. In these ecumenical days it may easily come to
supersede the well-known divisions between Papalist and
Protestant, Catholic and Evangelical, High Church and Low
Church. It would be a much more realistic demarcation than
the quite outmoded system still maintaining its tottering
fences between the various denominations of the post-
Reformation period.

The possibility that the factualists and symbolists may find
some *modus vivendi* and still manage to live together in the
same organisation should not be allowed to disguise from us
the extent to which a thorough-going symbolism would
depart from traditional Christianity. It may be true that the
psychological values they each aim at are the same, but the
means by which they seek to achieve them are very different.

The symbolist avoids the scandal of particularity. He is
prepared to support the whole Christian ethos in general, if
he is not asked to accept any historical fact in particular. An

exception should be made in favour of the crucifixion, which he accepts because it does not involve any irruption into space and time by what used to be called the 'supernatural'. The empty tomb has been replaced by a 'resurrection event', and symbolises the continued life of Christ beyond the grave. The ascension has disappeared altogether or is retained merely as a symbol to emphasise Christ's victory over sin and evil. Whitsun is a pictorial representation of the purifying and vitalising operation of the Holy Spirit.

It is believed that this method of interpreting the New Testament will commend Christianity to modern men because it does not demand credulous acceptance of any precise or datable explosion of the infinite into the finite, of the universal into space, of the eternal into time. This means of course that there is no tangible or obvious evidence of either an Incarnation or a Revelation beyond what is ordinary and commonplace. To the observer this must appear to imply that all the foundation elements of what has hitherto been understood as historical Christianity have disappeared.

It is true that the symbolists still continue to repeat the creed, and this they must obviously do *ex animo*. But it must take a good deal of esoteric explanation to make the creed fit their allegorising attitude to traditional history. However, the fact that they can still repeat the creed makes it possible for them and the factualists to dwell together in unity. It will be for the latter to see that, under this possibly corrosive influence, their carefully nurtured historical religion does not decline into a mere philosophy.

It cannot be denied that to some extent all have found in the allegorists' method some relief from a too oppressive literalism. Where a slavish interpretation had produced a result too absurd or too shocking to be easily reconciled with the character of God's word, recourse has often been had to a symbolic explanation. That, after all, had been Plato's way of dealing with the classical myths, and Philo as well as some of the rabbis had used the same method with the Old Testament.

Consequently in the early medieval Church a threefold method of interpretation was recognised: literal, moral, and allegorical. But the two latter were not generally intended to do away with the first: rather they found for it a more worthy meaning at a more exalted level. Thus the obviously physical love songs in *Canticles* became symbols of the ecstatic union between God and his chosen people, or between Christ and his Church. The passage of the Red Sea became the symbol of the deliverance of the Elect Race from every evil that would destroy it, and so of salvation. The utterly savage and inhuman destruction of children commended in Psalm 137:9 became a symbol of what an earnest man will do with the children of his own evil imagination.

The New Testament gives a certain authority for this method of interpretation. Jonah's three days' entombment in the belly of the 'whale' is there interpreted as a foreshadowing of Jesus' burial in the grave (Jonah 1:17; Matt. 12:40). The rock that pursued the wandering Israelites in the wilderness and provided them with a constant supply of water is seen as none other than Christ himself (I Cor. 10:4). The unnamed mother of a child in the troubled days of Ahaz becomes a symbol of the mother of the Messiah and so ultimately of Mary the mother of Jesus (Matt. 1:23).

Christian apologists cannot deny this use of the allegorical method. What they must do is to ask whether there are any limits beyond which it cannot be allowed to go. Of course, if it is to be assumed that the original statement is a statement of fact before and after the allegory is applied, there is no need from this point of view to impose any limit on allegorisation except that of appropriateness to the occasion. We are here, however, concerned rather with the kind of allegory that dissolves the original into an insubstantial picturisation. Are there not facts of Christian history that ought on no account to be submitted to this kind of transformation?

One takes it for granted that the flesh and blood existence of Jesus is such a fact. There are probably not many who would be prepared to accept Christianity, as a viable faith if (*per impossibile*) it were proved that no such person as Jesus of Nazareth ever lived. How far we must be prepared to go beyond that is a matter for discussion. Practically everyone would be anxious to include the crucifixion as established fact. After all there is nothing supernatural in such an event. But it must be noted that at least the meaning attributed to the death—the part it had to play in man's salvation—is 'supernatural'. Here it is possible to draw a clear line between the event and the *kerygma*, between the fact and its proclamation as means of salvation. It is very doubtful, however, whether either would have remained long in the Christian tradition without the other. If there had been no such event, the original proclamation would have been stillborn. And so, in effect, would have been the event, had there been no proclamation.

The resurrection of Jesus occupies a different position, because it is generally taken, as described in the New Testament, to imply both a resuscitation of the body and a radical change in the physical condition of Jesus. Upon that event a great deal of doctrine has been built. In other words here is an instance where both the alleged fact and the interpretation are supernatural. Although it must be remembered that behind both the resuscitation and the transformation lies the quite simple fact of the empty tomb.

The present tendency of scholarship is to get rid of the supernatural element in the case by refusing to accept the story of the empty tomb. But that refusal we have already seen to be unnecessary and unscientific. It further proposes to get rid of the supernatural element in the alleged resuscitation and transformation by supposing that the resurrection stories are mere picturesque ways of affirming that Jesus was alive in whatever sense post-mortem life may be predicated of any dead person. This extraordinarily jejune teaching eviscerates the resurrection of Jesus of any special or unique significance. On this view all we can say at the historical level is that certain people who believed that Jesus was dead, now affirmed their conviction that he was alive.

A proportion of scholars who are not prepared to eliminate the supernatural altogether from the process of contingent causation are left facing the question what they are to believe with regard to the considerable number of alleged miracles that cluster like satellites around the great occurrences such as the birth and crucifixion of Jesus, to say nothing of the signs and wonders that attended the general course of his ministry. The answer must be that as historians they must examine the character of the documentary evidence. Here again the rule must apply that no amount of material evidence can prove the intervention of the supernatural, but there may well be occasions when such evidence as we have may seem to make a supernatural cause the most likely hypothesis.

To examine the question of the credibility of miracles would require a volume in itself. It would take us too far afield at this time to add to the works of Headlam, Richardson and others. We need merely note that, for those who do not rule out in advance the possibility of divine intervention in human affairs, there still remain some severe tests before they can accept a wonder-story as historically reliable. The candid inquirer must ask such questions as the following:

(1) What exactly does the narrator say?
(2) Is his story meant to be taken literally or allegorically?
(3) What evidence is there in other New Testament documents or elsewhere to support his account?
(4) Is any 'natural' explanation of the event possible?
(5) Does the event, if inexplicable by known natural law, fit in with what we understand as the 'scheme of salvation'?

As I have suggested elsewhere[1] the answers to those questions will help us to distinguish sharply between the general sobriety of the New Testament and the exuberance of the Apocryphal Gospels. They will also reveal that some of the New Testament 'wonders' are much more strongly attested than others, so that in some instances we must at least suspend judgment before rejecting them. They may even help us to decide how far we should be justified in making the act of faith necessary to accept, as factually true, events that cannot be 'proved' by the natural reason alone.

The present situation in respect of this subject is complicated by the existence of a solid body of devout opinion which refuses to agree that any positive statement of Holy Writ is questionable. This strongly entrenched position its supporters refuse to leave under any pretext. One cannot help feeling a certain sympathy with their determination. After all, if one begins to hesitate about any one alleged fact, where is doubt to stop? We have already seen in this book how far it can go—even to the surrender of every biographical statement about Jesus except that of his actual birth and death.

But the penalty of this position is that it takes New Testament studies right out of the field of scholarship. It contradicts the principle with which we began, that we must be prepared to read the Bible 'like any other book'. Once we have begun to read in that way we must be struck from time to time by statements that seem out of keeping with the general sobriety of the rest. St. Matthew 27:52, for instance, with its story of opening tombs and bodies of saints wandering in the streets of Jerusalem, or Acts 19:12 with its account of handkerchiefs and aprons being produced from the body of St. Paul: such items must make it impossible for most readers to take up an entirely intransigent position. And once we have begun to question, we must continue to do so until we have reached a conclusion.

Not that we shall always be able to say precisely what happened. Who, for example, would be prepared to say exactly what occurred within the sealed tomb on the night when Jesus 'rose again'? However impatient we may sometimes feel with critics who appear to create difficulties for the sake of having something to say, there remains enough unsettled business to engage all the skill and energy we can bring to it.

In short, the present situation is as 'open-ended' as it could well be. At the one extreme it includes those who would like to avoid the issue altogether, and at the other those who adopt a position of almost complete agnosticism. In between are the various grades of those who believe that the ultimate aims of faith and reason are the same and that both can find satisfaction in a devout and scholarly study of the scriptures.

Notes

[1] Wand, *The Life of Jesus Christ* (2nd ed., Methuen, 1961), p. 130.

6

The Main Question

We have tried to throw a little light on the present situation of historical studies in their relation to the supernatural element in the scriptures. It has been seen that, even among professing Christians, opinions vary from an extreme historical scepticism to a readiness to examine open-mindedly each case as it arises. We have not left out of sight the very devout section of Christians who hold what is generally known as the 'fundamentalist' position, and who are supposed to accept every word of the scriptures as literally true. Their position is not arrived at by reason, nor is it necessarily supported by reason. It is believed presumably to be the immediate result of a God-given conviction, and is therefore impervious to the corrosive influence of ratiocination. For the holders of such a position there can be little interest in the kind of inquiry we are conducting.

For the rest of us the main question must always be whether any historical evidence can ever be sufficient to prove a supernatural event. Put thus simply and crudely the question can only be answered once again by a decided negative. It would appear that an alternative explanation of a 'natural' type is always possible. When some thought that a voice spoke to Jesus out of heaven (John 12:29), others thought that it thundered. And so it will always be. Jesus himself appears to some as Son of God while to others he is the mere 'carpenter's son'. The case for the supernatural is always open to argument.

What we have said so far emphasises the dilemma in which religious historians are placed. Recognising the difficulty of arriving at historical facts, and granted the amount of para-history, myth, symbol and legend, mixed up with them, the scholars are hard pressed to find any solid basis on which to build their scheme of religion. What we have to ask now is whether there is any escape from this dilemma.

1

One possible way out, which has received far less attention than it deserves, was proposed in 1958 by Dr. Philip Bagby in his book *Culture and History*.[1] He thinks that history should be far less concerned than it is with individual acts and events and should develop a stronger feeling for successive stages of culture. He feels that, while the single episode has become extremely uncertain as foundation material, a whole layer of civilisation would be much more secure.

One is reminded of the thirteenth-century builders of Salisbury Cathedral, who, fearing disaster if they rested the weight of their superstructure on single pillars in direct contact with the marshy soil, laid down a broad flat wall and rested their pillars upon it, thus distributing the thrust, and securing at least six centuries of stability for their magnificent pile.

So Dr. Bagby would distribute the weight of the historical argument. "It is my hope that historical researchers will give up their futile attempts to establish the exact truth as to individual actions in the past, and seek more and more to investigate, as far as possible, every aspect of the culture of every period." Or again, "the proposition that the comparative study of the development of ideas and values is the key to the understanding of history seems to be an inescapable deduction" (pp. 128 and 191).

It is hardly likely that such a method would be regarded as wholly satisfactory by Christian historians. After all, their religion is very much concerned with one particular person. They are bound to be interested, not only in the actual existence of Jesus of Nazareth, but in every detail they can establish about him. It would be too much to ask the Christian scholar to relinquish this search in order to give himself up entirely to tracing the development of ideas and culture.

Nevertheless Dr. Bagby's suggestion could provide a very useful ancillary method for the Christian student. There is an echo of it in Professor Nineham's favourite argument that, however hard it may be to establish particular facts about Jesus, there can be no doubt that the portrait of him belongs to the first century A.D. The picture fits in precisely to the background of that special period. However unusual he may be, Jesus in that setting is not an incongruous figure. And that, it is implied, is a strong argument for his historicity. "Whatever qualifications have to be made, the Jesus of Mark, with the language he uses, the traditional parabolic method of teaching he employs, the claims he makes, and the hostilities he arouses, is beyond any doubt basically a figure of early first-century Palestine and not an invention of late first-century Rome" (*Pelican Gospel Commentary S. Mark*, 1963, p. 50).

For those who are concerned in the attempt to rehabilitate the prestige of history this concession may not seem to amount to very much, *mais c'est toujours quelque chose*. It is a beginning: if it is not a foundation, it is at least pretty firm ground in which a foundation can be laid. Should anyone complain that it is much too general and vague, we can remind him that the general is made up of particulars. When it is said that the figure of Jesus, as it is painted in the New Testament, fits into the known background of his times, it is implied that in a multitude of details what is said of him agrees with what is known or credibly surmised of that particular epoch. When expert historians acquiesce in such a judgment, they are in fact accepting the detailed parallelism although they might not be willing to assert its justification in every particular. We are therefore justified in assuming at the outset that we are on fair historical ground.

2

Another route taken by many today is to divide sharply between the *mythos* and the *kerygma*[2] of the New Testament and practically to ignore the former while putting all the emphasis on the latter. This method offers the advantage of getting rid of all the awkward questions about the historicity of detailed events in the life of Jesus while occupying oneself with the proclamation of the apostles and first-generation Christians. It implies basing one's faith on the preaching of the early Church rather than on any chronological outline of the life of Christ.

The Main Question

Kerygma, we should note, means both the proclamation of the good news and the good news proclaimed. The good news is that the ancient prophecies have at last been fulfilled in the person of Jesus Christ, by whose life, death and resurrection the way of salvation has been freely opened to all who would turn from their evil ways and accept the gift of grace and the guidance of the Holy Spirit. The *kerygma* was thus not so much an assertion of dogmatic truth, or an appeal for historical investigation, as a challenge to faith or trust. It is claimed that this was the original 'gospel' or good news. We must try to understand in what sense this could be true.

We know from the gospels that even the people who knew Jesus personally and were his companions in the great events of his life 'understood none of these things at the first; but when Jesus was glorified . . .' (John 12:16). The shock of the knowledge that the Crucified was actually alive produced in them, if not a changed mentality, at least a quite new way of looking at the story of his earthly life. Under the genius of St. Paul and his school this new interpretation was built up into a scheme of salvation which was already being preached before the gospels were written.

The converts who accepted this proclamation of good news had, for the most part, never heard Jesus or seen him. They received the *kerygma* before hearing the *mythos*. It is suggested that we should not be going far wrong if we followed their example. In fact we are forcibly reminded that the apostle to the Gentiles deliberately advised that course. "Though we have known Christ after the flesh, yet now we know him so no more" (2 Cor. 5:16). We can take the point but refuse to let it imply that the historical details of Jesus'

59

life are unimportant. As the context shows, to 'know Christ after the flesh' means to judge him by pre-resurrection standards. His triumph over death has made all the difference in the Christian's understanding of him. The *New English Bible* makes this clear: "Worldly standards have ceased to count in our estimate of any man; even if once they counted in our understanding of Christ, they do so now no longer. When anyone is united to Christ, there is a new world; the old order has gone, and a new order has already begun."

It would be manifestly unfair to take the apostle's argument as implying that the historical events of the life of Christ were of no importance. The obvious determination with which he presses home the detailed facts about such events as the institution of the Lord's Supper, the burial, and the resurrection, shows that for St. Paul at least the *kerygma* sprang logically out of the *mythos*. No doubt he emphasises the former more than the latter, but that is because it is his business so to do, just as it is the evangelists' business to reverse the process and narrate the actual or alleged events. As it turns out, the distinction is a little blurred because the evangelists wished to take part in the proclamation. They were not content to provide the bare bones of historical fact, but supplied also some flesh and blood of interpretation. They presented the figure of Jesus so as to draw all men unto him.

Our difficulty is to show precisely how justifiably the meaning relies upon the facts. Is the Christ of the *kerygma* really identifiable with the original Jesus behind the gospel story? There can be little doubt that he is so identifiable as the gospels now stand. But we have seen that the gospels

themselves offer, not a plain, unvarnished tale but an interpretation; and if that interpretation is not influenced by St.
Paul himself, it most certainly is by the post-resurrection
thoughts of the primitive Church. This must mean that the
gospel narrative already partakes of the nature of *kerygma*.

We are thus thrown back upon the long-standing *Quest
for the Historical Jesus*, a quest which, in spite of all the
warnings about not knowing Christ after the flesh, is being
renewed in our own day. We may well think that the future
lies with such renewed research rather than with the illogical
acceptance of the *kerygma* as somehow historically respectable while the *mythos* is not. It is surely misguided to say to
oneself 'at least we are on safe practical ground in affirming
that this is what the first generation of Christians proclaimed', if you are not sure that the apostles themselves
were on safe historical grounds in affirming certain alleged
facts as the basis of their propaganda. Of what use is the
apostolic belief to us, if it was not founded on fact? We must
still find some means of filling the alleged gap between the
Jesus of history and the Christ of faith.

Therefore, although a good deal has been learnt in the
process of defining *kerygma* and contrasting it with the
purely narrational element in the gospel story, the method
cannot be regarded as affording a satisfactory way of escape
from our dilemma over the problem of history.

3

A third suggestion, which has certain affinities with the
last, is to abandon the search for facts altogether and to rely
entirely upon values. This is generally regarded as the

expedient of the Roman Catholic modernists of the late nine-teenth century. Although the imputation is denied in respect of such biblical and historical scholars as Loisy and Tyrrell, it is certainly true of the more philosophical section headed by Blondel.

The theory was based on the teaching of Ritschl and Troeltsch. It begins by asserting that there is no fact without value, and ends by suggesting, in effect, that once you have the value you need no longer bother about the fact. Indeed it sometimes seems to confuse value with fact. There is a curious footnote in William Temple's *Christus Veritas*, p. 113. Speaking of the Incarnation, Temple says of Jesus, "He cannot really have the value of God unless He is God." But to suggest that nothing can have the value of something which it actually is not seems to fly in the face of a good deal of psychological experience. On a crowded night a settee may have the value of a bed; yet the upholsterer would contend that it remains a settee.

It is commonly held that the Catholic modernists built a good deal upon this theory of value. The argument ran that if the traditional system of Church dogma and practice had the desired effect in the psychological experience of the believer, that is to say, if it effected his salvation, then there was no need to worry about the historical basis of the system. This attitude seemed plausible enough, and no doubt things did often work out like that, not only for simple folk, but even for those who had sufficient knowledge of movements of the psyche to reason out the case for themselves. The weight of one's conceptual environment will often carry one with it even without a conscious submission to historical claims.

But it is extremely doubtful, even apart from the question

of intellectual honesty, whether such a method could prove a permanent way out of our present dilemma. Few men can keep their mental processes in completely separate compartments. The creed weds history and doctrine together in indissoluble bonds. One who doubts the history will soon begin to doubt the doctrine. And once the 'little devil doubt' has found a lodgement in the foundations the whole erection, however elaborate, will be in danger of destruction. If such is the case of the individual, the case of believing society as a whole is closely parallel.

It was the recognition of this danger that gave rise to the papal repression of Modernism in the decree *Lamentabili* and the encyclical *Pascendi* in 1907. The effect of these measures was to drive open-minded discussion underground. How widespread that discussion nevertheless continued to be was shown in the second Vatican Council, which astonished the world by the freedom with which some at least of its members criticised every distinctive element of traditional Catholicism. Since then the Roman Church has furnished many liberal considerations of our immediate problem. Owing to the immense solidity of the Tridentine doctrinal system and the totalitarian character of its discipline, it is particularly tempting for Roman scholars to think that it is possible to preserve values while remaining uncertain of facts, but later developments within the Roman Church have already shown the precarious nature of such a position.

In religion, of all spheres of human life, complete honesty and scrupulous sincerity are necessary. In this respect it is impossible to rob Peter in order to pay Paul. We cannot improve our hold upon Christian doctrine and practice while deducting from our belief in its historical evidence. It is inevitable that if we lost our grasp of the historical facts we should soon lose our grip of the Christian life as a whole. As St. Paul said, if Christ be not raised, we are of all men the most miserable; our belief in any kind of moral resurrection will be undermined and we shall be yet 'in our sins'.

At the same time this style of argument is far from being without importance. It helps to remind us of the value of 'value'. For a generation that is only just escaping from the more dry-as-dust methods of historical criticism it is an immense relief to be once again made aware of a world in which spiritual and moral realities are paramount. We are no longer satisfied with bare facts. Even if we have uncovered them, we realise that we have not come to the end of our quest until we have considered their effects. We are not satisfied with knowing what *truly* happened: we must translate it into a knowledge of what really happened.

4

A fourth method of escape from our dilemma is the one that seems to have won most favour in recent years among the professional theologians, although it has by no means been accepted by the rank and file of believers. It is the theory associated with the name of Rudolph Bultmann, namely that we should frankly recognise the predominant part played by the *kerygma* in formulating the thought of the New Testament and accept the full consequences of such a recognition.[3] Its books were not written from the point of view of the modern scholar but rather from that of the mission preacher. Its contents are essentially a challenge to every man to accept the position of a penitent sinner relying wholly upon the free gift of God for salvation.

The suggestion continues that, once this essential characteristic of the scriptures is grasped, we lose all need to be anxious about the historical details of the narrative. Provided that the evidence is sufficient for the all-important facts that Jesus lived and died, we do not need anything else: it is solely on the basis of those two essential facts that the whole inspiring system of Christian doctrine has been erected. Much of it has come down to us in the mythological terms of the first century, and can be amended or discarded without loss, so long as the fundamental challenge is preserved. But what is more important is that we are no longer tied to shifting judgments of the so-called historical details.

About this ingenious attempt to solve the difficulty several things must be said. First, for Christianity, as it has been traditionally understood, it is certainly not enough merely to know that a person named Jesus lived and died. It is just as important to know what kind of person he was. When Paul was struck down by the sudden voice on the Damascus road his first question was "Who art thou, Lord?" Christians have gone on asking that question ever since. It is no good telling them that they have a deliverer, if they do not know what kind of deliverer he is. Their very trust in him depends upon the answer to that question.

Again, Bultmann's reply that it is quite impossible to arrive at an agreed portrait of Jesus since it would have to depend upon a multitude of details which are themselves in dispute, is quite unsatisfactory. No one would deny that there have been many different portraits of the Nazarene. Not only each generation but each individual has drawn the likeness according to particular and peculiar tastes. But this does not eliminate the fact that behind all the portraits there is still a common and recognisable character.

If some of this characterisation is derived from the *kerygma*, it still remains to be seen whether it is in agreement with the basic tradition of the synoptic gospels. That is a judgment of the greatest difficulty. The documents have to be examined with the most meticulous care, and it cannot be said that there is complete agreement yet as to the original elements of the tradition. Some scholars are happy to think that they can trace fragments of the gospels to Jesus himself, while others think that they can penetrate no further back than (at best) the second generation of the Christian community. At such an interval there must have been plenty of opportunity for interpretation and actual distortion. In such circumstances it is not easy to say how the original oral narrative has been affected by the *kerygma* or, for the matter of that, to discover and separate the one clearly and decisively from the other.

It is therefore not possible to accept the distinction between *kerygma* and *mythos* as a way out of our difficulty. Nevertheless we can be grateful to the Bultmann school for emphasising once again the true character of the gospels as not a historical exercise so much as a challenge to faith. No one has taught us more clearly than the Christian existentialists that the gospel is intended to pull men up short, to compel them to consider their individual situation before God, and so to bring about a genuine acceptance of the new life offered in Christ.

5

A quite different way of escape is suggested by those historians who think that they can find traces of an over-ruling plan in history. It need hardly be said that this view is by no means universally accepted. H. A. L. Fisher, for instance, in the famous preface to his *History of Europe*[4] said that he could find no evidence among the multifarious data of events for any guiding principle. Hegel, however, long before, had propounded his theory of a constantly repeated rhythmic progress in history from thesis to antithesis and on to synthesis. Many who have not been willing to subscribe wholeheartedly to such an abstraction have nevertheless often found it a useful three-pronged fork with which to turn over the material at their disposal.

In more recent times Spengler in his *Decline of the West*[5] has seen in history a perpetual circular movement, a nation of culture climbing upwards to the height of its ambition and power and then beginning to decline until it has reached again the point at which it began. This process had already been adumbrated by ancient Greek philosophers, and he regarded it as inevitable. When asked what the individual could do if he knew that his country was in a state of decline, he replied that he could remain at his post without flinching, like the Roman sentry at the gate of Pompeii. It is generally believed that it was rebellion against this fatalistic teaching which led to the catastrophic reaction of Hitlerite youth in Germany.

A complete antithesis to the determinist teaching of Spengler, while still allowing for his notion of a rhythmic movement in history, is provided by Arnold Toynbee in his monumental *Study of History*.[6] He dismisses the notion of inevitability altogether, and sees in the rise of nations the result of challenge and response. At every epoch circumstances arise which require, in order to be adequately handled, the utmost skill and determination. The way in which a nation responds to such a challenge determines its immediate fate. If it concentrates its forces and summons up all its energies to overcome the threatening disaster, it will emerge so much stronger and so much nearer the peak of its destiny. If it fails, it becomes so much weaker and declines towards dissolution.

Such an outline of the plan of history may be regarded either as a truism or as an unprovable theory. In Toynbee's case it was supported by such a vast coverage of historical judgments that it gave the specialists an opportunity to attack him on every section of a very wide front. In the tactical assault the general strategy seemed to lose importance. The modern historian does not much care for generalisation. Perhaps the most important result of Toynbee's effort from our present point of view was that at least one considerable historian was shown to find evidence of a plan in universal history and so to leave the door open for belief in a providential ordering of affairs.

Much the same opinion might be expressed with regard to Professor Butterfield and the lectures he gave to the University of Cambridge in 1948 called *Christianity and History*. He, however, does not see history working itself out in some planned progress towards perfection. If the goal is in the eternal sphere, "then those who rest their ultimate beliefs in progress are climbing a ladder which may be as vertical as they claim it to be, but which in reality is resting on nothing at all. If there is a meaning in history, therefore, it lies not in the systems and organisations that are built over long periods, but in something more essentially human, something in each personality considered for mundane purposes as an end in himself" (p. 90). Thus the prominence that Toynbee gives to the state Butterfield gives to the individual: there is still room for the activity of an overruling Providence; but whereas for Toynbee the aim is the production of the Kingdom of God, for Butterfield it is the production of a universe of saints.

Here again we find that we are given no certain clue. Events, however carefully we teazle them out, fail to lead irresistibly to the conclusion of a divine ordering of history. The stream does not bear an obvious plan on its surface. There may be indications of it, but only such as require the eye of faith rather than the skill of the researcher in order to be adequately observed. One is reminded of St. Augustine's reply to those who argued that if there were a Providence then he would immediately punish the wicked and reward the good. Not so, replied the Bishop of Hippo, for then everyone would be logically forced into virtue, and a compulsory virtue is no virtue at all.[7] Here again then we must face the possibility of doubt.

6

It will have been noticed that some of the ways out of our difficulty already considered apply to comparatively detailed issues (as for instance the suggestion to discard the biographical narrative in the gospels in favour of the *kerygma*), while others relate to the broad general sweep of history (such as the views just discussed as to the recognition of a purposeful plan in the ordering of events). This discrepancy between the particular and the universal in the development of our theme makes us ask whether we ought not to consider the basic question of methodology. Is it possible that we have adopted the wrong attitude to the whole question? Are we sure that we are going about our task in the right way?

It is interesting to notice how often the secular historians are wont to twit their theological colleagues with over-anxiety. They wonder why we are so deeply suspicious of every document we have to handle and why we are never willing to give to any statement the benefit of the doubt.

It is certainly true that the deepest possible suspicion is regarded by many as the only proper attitude to adopt when approaching ancient documents, especially those concerned with the beginnings of Christianity. It is rather like the stern warning of the detective in a police novel: 'All of you are under suspicion until this matter is cleared up.' There is no doubt that the prevailing mood among the most vocal section of New Testament scholars at the moment is one of historical scepticism.

An amusing instance of it occurs unexpectedly in Van Harvey's otherwise able and well-informed book *The Historian and the Believer*.[8] He is arguing against his colleagues' acceptance of the empty tomb. "There is," one of them had affirmed, "much to be said in support of it and little definite and convincing evidence against it: it is therefore probably historical." This stings Harvey to contemptuous wrath. "How could a critical historian argue that since much can be said for it and no convincing evidence

70

exists against it, it is probably historical?" That retort puts the all-too-common attitude in a nutshell. We may well ask Harvey how a critical historian can do anything else than decide on the evidence before him—unless indeed he already holds some secret which will invalidate in advance any evidence that can be brought in favour of the phenomenon in question?

The plain fact is that in this kind of argument the sceptic is not functioning as a historian at all. He starts with the assumption that there could be no corporal resurrection since that would have been against nature; and so he argues that the tomb could not possibly have been empty (although as a matter of fact, it could have been emptied by quite other means than a bodily resurrection). That is to say, he rejects the evidence because he does not like a conclusion that it may be used to support.[9]

A canon of judgment in this respect has lately been laid down by Samuel Laeuchli in *The Serpent and the Dove* (p. 115). He is dealing with the story of Constantine's vision before the battle of the Milvian Bridge and addressing himself to those scholars who, because they think the purport of the vision highly improbable, therefore deny that there was any vision at all. "It is a grave mistake," says Laeuchli, "to attack historicity when one actually wants to attack the content."

These instances must serve to show how difficult it is to obtain a purely objective judgment in matters involving historical criticism. Every historian must examine himself to see whether he is reaching his conclusions on the evidence before him or on some quite extraneous position already reached. All of us do in fact from time to time follow the latter procedure: we reject a multitude of stories because they fly in the face of what we already hold to be credible. If we are good historians, we shall be ready to acknowledge our natural bias.

These illustrations show also how important is the fundamental attitude with which we approach our present subject. If our minds are made up at the outset that there is no such thing as the supernatural and no such process as an intervention of the eternal in time and space, then we shall rule out in advance all allegedly historical evidence in their favour, or we shall try to show that the evidence, although good in itself, is really evidence for something else. In any case it is quite certain that we cannot just accept any historical evidence as sufficient of itself as if it functioned in a vacuum. We are, as we are so often reminded, mature men in a world come of age. Whatever that may mean, it includes the fact that there are some limits to our credulity: history is not the only criterion of reality: its evidence must lie within the bounds of antecedent possibility before we can accept it as final.

Yet, provided that there is no diriment impediment, belief must follow the historical argument. And of course the converse is true: historical argument, if accepted, must lead to belief. Faith could not sustain itself if there were not believed to be some substratum of fact upon which it can rest. Christology itself needs the historical datum: 'suffered under Pontius Pilate'. As Teilhard de Chardin said in a memorable sentence of *Le Milieu Divin*, "the Mystical Christ, the universal Christ of St. Paul, has neither meaning nor value in our eyes except as an expansion of the Christ who was born of Mary and who died upon the cross."

What we need is a sympathetic attitude to the whole historical process from the primitive myth to the latest entry in the statute book. We are not here to treat narratives of the past as if they were prisoners in the dock, but as friendly guides and counsellors. Such do not disclose everything, and they may be quite mistaken; but each makes some suggestion, which must be subject to examination. Above all we must be prepared to continue with our examination and never give it up as a hopeless task.

7

If we may cross over for a moment from the academic to the pastoral field, we may repeat that a temporary way of escape from the dilemma would be to 'let both grow together until harvest', to recognise the presence of both history and para-history in our documents and work with both until in the slow process of debate and research some agreed solution to the riddle can be found. After all, that is in effect what happens today. The Christian who owes no ecclesiastical allegiance, who belongs to no special 'Church', in so far as he is interested in the question at all, does not feel himself tied to any particular statement of belief; and so he is not vitally concerned with the precise amount of factual history that lies behind his somewhat jejune profession of faith. History and para-history exist side by side in his own mental survey. The average person probably accepts the main events as recounted in the gospels and feels uncommitted about the minor.

Among those, however, who do acknowledge a particular ecclesiastical allegiance the division does not come within the individual conscience so much as within the community as a whole, separating those who still contend for a completely historical basis for their religion from those who accept as inevitable the mixture of history and myth. This division cuts right across other well-known ecclesiastical boundaries. Believers who take the roughly fundamentalist position with regard to the scriptures are to be found in both the Catholic and the Evangelical camps: and so also are such as adopt the more liberal attitude.

Among the more liberal members there is a great variety of views according to the amount of verifiable fact that is believed to be discoverable in the record. Some will accept nothing as historical beyond the bare facts of the existence and death of Jesus, while at the opposite extreme others are prepared to accept almost everything in the record while allowing for the possibility of doubt in a few exceptional cases. The variations and consequent confusion are almost endless.

So far there has been in recent times no full-scale attack by any one section upon another. There have been one or two heresy charges against individuals, but they have served more to publicise *avant-garde* ideas than any other purpose. The last determined effort at forcible suppression of liberal opinion was the papal attack on modernism in the nineteenth century. As was suspected at the time, the main result of this effort was to drive speculative theology underground. Recent events, especially the second Vatican Council, have shown how much progress the study of criticism has made in the Roman Catholic communion during the last sixty years, in spite of the lack of publicity.

Magna est veritas et praevalet. Those who are on the side

of God need not fear the truth. Indeed it is part of their religion to seek it. This is a truism and is only repeated here in order to support the suggestion that in the present state of knowledge it is not wise to insist, even in Church circles, on an *ex animo* belief in the literal historicity of all the articles of the creed. While the majority of Christian people can still affirm their faith in the traditional manner, there are others who can accept the historical elements only after the manner of allegory or symbol. The distinction may seem of little vital concern to the professor in his study, but it seems a matter of life and death to the pastoral minister and to many thousands of the faithful laity. Nevertheless, it should be recognised that over-precision in matters of faith creates more difficulties than it resolves.

It would seem that for the time being at least the actual recitation of the creed must be the confessional bond uniting all parties. The sense in which it is recited must be the responsibility of the individual conscience. This has been very generally recognised in recent times in respect of some at least of the more controverted of the historical articles. For instance, there have not been many bishops in recent years who have refused an ordination candidate on the ground that he did not 'believe the Virgin Birth'. If the candidate is prepared to make the statutory declaration, no question has been asked. No doubt he himself would find the situation more difficult if he could not accept as historically accurate the statement 'rose again the third day'. But even then, if he accepted the creed and did not himself raise the question of interpretation, it is unlikely that any special inquiry would be made. After all, a very wide liberty is already recognised as allowable in respect of the Thirty-nine Articles.

In the present state of intellectual progress the principle of 'live and let live' seems not only the most charitable but also the most practicable. It allows for honest and fearless inquiry and leaves the way open for ultimate arrival at a common conclusion. One must admit that the situation would be easier if both sides refrained from provocative smartness. Phrases like 'possible impossibility', 'religionless Christianity', 'death of God' are either meaningless paradoxes or else require so much explaining as to be worthless for ordinary argument. The usual excuse given for coining them, 'It is necessary to jolt people into wakefulness', is even a little impertinent, suggesting, as it does, that only those who are clever enough to frame such epigrams are already aware of what is going on in the world of thought. Those who say that we ought not to 'receive one who is weak in the faith to doubtful disputations', and who ask that when new speculations are given publicity they should not be more provocatively expressed than is necessary, have at least a pastoral interest which should not be far from the heart of any theologian.

The question, however, is bound to arise how far institutionalised Christianity may allow demythologising of the creed to go. Is it to be possible in the case of every article, as apparently the 'God is dead' school would wish, or is it to be limited to the historical articles, or even to only minor ones among them? It would indeed be a break with traditional Christianity if we allowed every article to be relegated to the sphere of symbolism and did not insist upon a literal interpretation of any single one. This is at the moment a particularly serious question. We may have an opportunity to return to it towards the end of this book.

With a certain amount of sympathy and forbearance, scholars, students, and intelligent lay folk should be able to live and think together in common helpfulness. Such mutual accommodation will at least provide a practical way out of the apparent impasse into which our researches have led us. But this is very far from suggesting that it provides a means of finally bridging the intellectual gap between the realists and the fantasists. That struggle must still be played out to the end. The literalists will never be content with a mere *als ob*: they will always want to know whether events truly happened, and they will always be anxious not to build their historical faith on too narrow or limited a basis of interpretation. The only solution that will satisfy them is one that will bring the two horns of the dilemma together. They will want to have it both ways. We admit the cogency of their plea, and turn again to see what can be done to meet their demand.

Notes

[1] Longmans, *passim*.

[2] *Kerygma*—the proclamation of Jesus as Saviour, as set out in the epistles and reflected in the gospels of the New Testament.

[3] Since we only know the *kerygma* from the New Testament, there is an obvious circle in this argument.

[4] Eyre and Spottiswoode, 1935.

[5] The English translation, 1926.

[6] O.U.P., 1934–54 (10 vols.).

[7] *City of God*, XX, 2.

[8] S.C.M., 1967, p. 109. The quotation is from von Campenhausen via Zahrnt. The original is translated in von Campenhausen, *Tradition and Life in the Church* (Collins, 1968), p. 77, by A. V. Littledale, as follows: "There is much that tells in its favour, and nothing definite or significant against it. It is therefore probably historical."

[9] We may quote von Campenhausen again, loc. cit. "If we test what is capable of being tested, we cannot, in my opinion, shake the story of the empty tomb and its early discovery."

7

The Historical Jesus

We come now to what is in the eyes of many the culminating point of our theme, the historicity of Jesus. The acceptance of Christianity as a historical religion is bound up for most people with the idea of its founder as a real, material, living, personal, objective figure. If the picture we have of Jesus is fact and not mirage, then we are on safe ground in claiming for Christianity a historical foundation. However far subsequent ages may have departed from his teaching, however far the current portrait of the Saviour may differ from the original, and however different the elaborate organisation of the Church may be from the simple fellowship of Jesus and his apostles, Christianity can nevertheless still claim an actual historical personage as its first founder and present inspiration.

It is true that there are some who wonder why we should bother about all this. What is important to them is the moral and spiritual teaching of Christianity. If that is good, then Christianity is well founded in its own right, no matter who was the originator of its teaching. That is (whatever may be the rationale that supports it) the practical attitude of some modern teachers. They feel themselves on solid ground with the religious and humanitarian values of Christianity; so they can afford to let the rest go.

But that really will not do. It is quite impossible so to separate value from fact, teaching from life. Christianity is far too closely bound up with the passion, death and resurrection of Jesus to be treated as if it existed only in thin air. The *kerygma* itself is largely an interpretation of the facts of Jesus' life and teaching. Withdraw him as an identifiable personality and little is left but a cabbalistic ethical teaching, suspended like Mahomet's coffin between heaven and earth, touching neither.

Besides, there is so much in the teaching that seems bizarre, idealistic, extreme, that few people would be able to accept it or support it on a purely utilitarian basis. They need to have a human figure firmly anchored in space and time, who has fully tested the teaching in his own experience, to commend it to them. They need some assurance as to the *bona fides* of that figure to help guarantee the trustworthiness of the teaching.

It is precisely such comfort and guidance that is offered us in the person of Jesus Christ. Many millions in the past and the present have accepted the Christian ethic on the assumption that Jesus is a historical figure whose existence has been fully guaranteed by all such evidence as is open to critical investigation. That means that he is not a myth or a legend or a symbol only, but just as real a participator in past events as Caesar Augustus, Napoleon or Hitler. It is true that, in recognising his full authority, Christian orthodoxy has claimed that this historic figure is both perfect man and perfect God. But that, whatever we may think of its truth, is a type of interpretation, which, as we have seen, goes beyond the limit of strict history. And in any case it is not of much value until we have settled the primary question whether this person ever really existed.

About the bare existence there is little room for doubt. Certainly there is not much contemporary evidence outside the New Testament—as is natural, considering that as far as the secular features of it are concerned the event was little more than a routine occurrence in a fairly remote province of the Roman Empire. But the New Testament evidence, beginning with St. Paul, who was already writing twenty years after Jesus' crucifixion, is quite sufficient to establish the fact. And as news of the fact begins to reverberate through the Empire it is caught up in eminently respectable secular writings both Jewish and pagan, to which Josephus and the younger Pliny are the best known contributors (although the difficulties about the text of Josephus are widely recognised). It can safely be said that no reputable academic authority of our own day rejects the historicity of Jesus.

It was perhaps natural that nineteenth-century historians, confident in the accuracy of historical method, should feel that if only they were diligent enough they would be able to establish exactly what kind of person this Jesus was. It was the age in which natural science by the strict application of observation and analysis had revolutionised ideas about the physical development of the world and of life upon it. Why should not the same kind of success be available in the historical field?

At that time the new method of critical history was coming into its own. Nowhere was it more vigorously applied than in the sphere of New Testament studies. The results were nearly as startling as they had been in the sphere of natural science. When the top-hamper of traditional beliefs and ecclesiastical customs was cleared away, the simple figure of an 'original' Jesus began to appear. The trouble was that it appeared in so many different forms. To Rénan Jesus was the starry-eyed Galilean peasant. To Harnack he was the sober teacher of an ethical piety. To Schweitzer he was the fanatical prophet of an apocalyptic eschatology.

In the failure to reach agreement as to the precise portrait left by the original purveyors of the first oral tradition, many scholars decided that it would be better to give up the chase. It is frequently pointed out that, under conditions of modern historical criticism, it is in any case impossible to write a 'life' of Jesus. Form criticism has quite properly divided the gospels into fragments, and it is contended that these fragments have been arranged, not necessarily in chronological order, but to fit some special design of the compiler. Nor can we feel any more secure about the discourses put into the mouth of Jesus. It was not the custom of ancient writers to bother overmuch about the accuracy of their quotations, and where the speeches of some great hero were concerned it was the habit of the author to compose them himself. So long as he reproduced the thought of the speaker or put down what the speaker might have been expected to say, he transgressed no rules of literary propriety.

What put the coping-stone on the structure of this argument was Bultmann's vivid assertion that in any case what is found in the gospels is the product of the thought of the first century, when, as far as scientific outlook is concerned, mankind was in its infancy. The gospel narrative could not be expected to stand up to the tests of modern criticism. Bultmann did not shrink from describing it as myth, though, as

we know, the word myth did not carry to him the same connotation of pure fiction as it did originally to an English
mind. Still it meant that if you wanted to get down to the
hard core of the gospel not much of the traditional account
would be left for modern use. In the process of demythologising one would lose the specifically Jewish elements such as
the Messiah, the Suffering Servant, the Kingdom of God and
the apocalyptic visions of the world to come. So also must be
discarded what was typically Hellenistic, such as the Virgin
Birth, the notion of the Word, and the sacraments derived
from mystery cults, together with the ideas associated with
the title *Kyrios* or Lord. Bultmann's opponents said that his
process was remarkably like that of peeling off the successive
layers of an onion until at the end one had nothing left. But
that was not quite true, because Jesus himself was left,
although one could not see his face.

The effects of Bultmann's criticism have penetrated deep
and spread far. While it has been recognised that he did not
entirely abandon the historical position, but rested his case
for Christianity on the actual existence and death of Jesus,
it is felt that in his rewriting of the story very little of the
traditional Jesus remains. The process rapidly spread from
the lecture-room to the pulpit, and a preacher might be
heard explaining to his puzzled congregation that, as he
could no longer feel certain that we had any reliably authentic
words of Jesus, he would take his text from St. Paul!

On a somewhat higher intellectual level than this last
the same attitude dominates Guignebert's *Jesus*.[1] "Nothing
of Jesus has survived save the memory of his existence and
the influence of his work on his immediate associates." In
spite of that, "the rise of the Galilean prophet marks the

beginning, however accidental, of the religious movement from which Christianity sprang. . . . Enthusiasm engendered Christianity but it was the enthusiasm of the disciples, not that of Jesus" (p. 538). Public opinion in England was hardly stirred by those German and French views until they seemed to be echoed by one of our own most respected scholars. R. H. Lightfoot concluded his *History and Interpretation in the Gospels*[2] with a reminiscence of a passage from Job, applying it to the person of Christ: "For all the inestimable value of the gospels, they yield us little more than a whisper of his voice; we trace in them but the outskirts of his ways." The author complained afterwards that his critics had taken him too literally. But at least he had made his contemporaries see accurately enough what was the tendency of current teaching.

It is likely that that tendency was just part of the historical scepticism of the time. Such scepticism was itself symbolic of the general reaction on the part of practically every art and science against what was regarded as the complacency of the previous generation. It is a singular fact that our own epoch is restless under every kind of authority, and that every department of thought is in doubt about its own foundations. That we should be re-examining the very basis of theology is symptomatic of the spirit of our times.

It is not always recognised that this is a repetitive feature of theological study. Nor is it remembered that such a re-thinking marked the very emergence of Christianity as a distinct religion. All scholars, however, are agreed that the 'resurrection' of Jesus, whatever is implied by the term, made a revolutionary change in the thought of the disciples. The gospels themselves tell us as much. "Those things understood not his disciples at the first: but when Jesus was glorified, then remembered they that these things were written of him" (John 12:16).

In the light of that event many doubts and misunderstandings were cleared away, but above all there began a marked change in the whole estimation of the person and character of Jesus. By the time Paul began to write, not only was Jesus widely recognised to have been more than human, but a systematic Christology was already beginning to emerge. This judgment colours all that the evangelists subsequently wrote. It was natural that they should interpret the life of Jesus by what they believed to be the confirmation of his divine nature in his resurrection.

The main effort of modern criticism has been to get behind these post-resurrection reflections and to discover as far as possible what original tradition had to say about Jesus before it was affected by this outstanding event. To disentangle the earliest stratum of tradition is by no means easy, if not altogether impossible.

It is generally supposed that Aramaisms embedded in the gospel narrative are an indication of early date, because Aramaic is the language that Jesus spoke. Yet if one gathers together the Aramaic words and phrases that remain, one cannot recognise in them any markedly different colour from that which characterises the New Testament picture of Jesus as a whole. *Talitha cumi; eli, eli, lama sabachthani; abba; maranatha* all seem to reflect a spirit of special relationship to God. The cry of despair from the cross is the quotation of a confirmed user of the Jewish hymn-book, and (if the Suffering Servant and the Messiah were identified) shows no incompatibility with the 'Lord, come'. In any case it is obvious that neither St. Paul nor the evangelists were conscious of any essential incompatibility between what they knew of Jesus of Nazareth and of the risen Lord.

It is true that the New Testament does itself record a gradually deepening comprehension on the part of the disciples of the true character of the Master. Peter's confession at Caesarea Philippi and the subsequent scene at the Transfiguration (whatever may have been its precise nature[3]) seem to have formed the highest peak of understanding before the resurrection. There is no attempt on the part of the evangelists to disguise the fact that there was a setback at the passion and crucifixion, but the recovery was all the greater in the relief that followed the news of the empty tomb. That there remains a certain simplicity and naïvety about the narrative shows that the evangelists were not so affected by Pauline thought as to have forgotten the first faltering steps and to write altogether anachronistically of the earliest period of Christological development.

It has to be noted too that a good deal is said in the gospels to the discredit of the disciples, about their slowness to believe and their general stupidity, which could hardly have been said by any romancer who was trying to glamorise the picture of early Christianity. We need not be surprised if there is a certain amount of reading post-resurrection thoughts back into the pre-resurrection period—indeed we should be highly suspicious if the narrative had been kept hygienically clean from any such infection—but on the whole the account reads simply and naturally. Even the slowness on the part of the public to comprehend the claim to Messiahship is not disguised but explained by the story, whether true or false, of the Messianic secret.

Of course the conceptual atmosphere of the gospels in many respects is not ours, particularly where the long-drawn-out contest with the Devil and the whole world of demons is concerned; but that gives the narrative all the greater air of verisimilitude. There can at least be no doubt that the hero is a Palestinian Jew of the early first century. The point in the factual sphere that gives the modern reader most trouble is the abundance of miracles. Even that is in keeping with the temper of the time in which the narrative was written, and to that extent helps in arguing for the writers' veracity. They are at least surely right in recording the *belief* that miracles actually took place.

In any case it is no use starting with the assumption that any breakthrough from the supernatural into the natural sphere is impossible, for that would make the whole discussion pointless. And it is always possible that some at least of the so-called miracles are now susceptible of explanation by natural (psychological) causes, and may be therefore on the way to authentication.

The question is still whether, coming to the subject with an open mind, it is more possible than some modern scholars have thought to reach the 'historical Jesus'. Goguel complained that the critics were demanding a certainty in this field which belonged only to the realm of 'religious intuition and faith'.[4] He thought that the current hyper-criticism was an extreme reaction against the infallibility that used to be attributed to the Bible. As an example of mistaken criticism he points out the absurdity of trying to prove the crucifixion a myth from the fact that Paul gives three different explanations of it. In 1 Cor. 2:8 he says that the death of Jesus was due to the government's ignorance of God's fore-ordained plan; next, Rom. 8 : 3 says it was in order that God might pass an adequate judgment on sin in our human nature; and finally, 1 Thess. 2 : 15 says that it was due to the Jews following their usual line of killing off their prophets and so preventing other nations from attaining salvation. This multiplication of explanations, says Goguel, so far from proving the whole thing a myth, is merely Paul's attempt to see the undoubted fact of the crucifixion from different points of view.

However that may be, and however unlikely it is that faith can ever attain absolute certainty (for if it did, it would surely be no longer faith), we can probably agree with Goguel that in this particular instance it would indeed be an example of hyper-criticism to try to prove the crucifixion a myth on such doubtful grounds. But a good deal of water has flowed under the bridges since Goguel, and the pace of the stream has quickened during the last generation. This has been the period noteworthy for the influence of Karl Barth and his dialectical theology and then of Bultmann and his demythologisation theory. Barth, who has had more influence in Scotland than in England, did not deny the results of criticism but made them ineffective by putting all the emphasis on revelation. Science, history, reason were of little significance beside the one overwhelming fact that God had spoken to man in Christ. Let man but listen to that voice and he would find that it carried its own authority with it. Noteworthy was the fact that Barth's original thesis was based, not upon the gospels, but upon St. Paul's Epistle to the Romans.[5]

Bultmann, who was Barth's pupil, wedded his master's insistence on the immediacy of God's self-revelation to the existentialist philosophy of Heidegger. But he had his own drastic way of dealing with the critical problems of the gospels. He became a pioneer of 'form criticism', which quite rightly split up the documents behind our gospels into separate pieces such as parables, miracle-stories, disputations, homiletic fragments, and compared them with similar examples from other literature of the period. The alleged effect was to show how little could be said with certainty to belong distinctively to the historical Jesus. Even so we must begin, at whatever cost, by getting rid of all mythical elements, and this, as we have already seen, according to Bultmann, means leaving singularly little for a historical foundation.

This theory, although it has appeared to many the *ne plus ultra* of academic criticism, was intended to effect a practical aim. It was applied to the New Testament in an effort to translate the gospel message into terms that would be meaningful to the intellectually adult person of today. That is, we must agree, an entirely worthy motive. It is good that we should try to delineate Jesus as he might appear if all that was the alleged product of his contemporary environment were torn away. What have we left when the Virgin Birth has gone, the angels, the voices from heaven, the miracles, the Son of Man, the Suffering Servant, the Messiah, the physical resurrection, the ascension? It must be admitted that there seems to have been little left for Bultmann of the historical Jesus but the birth and crucifixion. There was of course also the teaching, but that only comes to us at second hand, through the disciples, affected as they were by their belief in the resurrection.

One cannot help feeling that for the ardent demythologiser every perceptible trace of the supernatural has been eliminated. Admittedly it is no good argument to impugn the other side's motives. But however little we desire it, *a priori* motives are almost bound to steal into our thinking and affect our attitude on practically every question. Those who do not believe in any case that God declares his presence by influencing the course of cause and effect are bound from the outset to be prejudiced against any alleged instance of that kind of influence whether it be in nature or history.

But whether the decisions of contemporary critical inquiry are influenced by such unconscious motives or are the fair results of the rigid application of strictly scientific rules, it is clear that the Jesus of history as thus depicted does not bear upon his features the compelling sign of any supernatural character. That, of course, is because we have deliberately eliminated such signs as mythological.

If anyone feels unduly distressed by this conclusion, it may perhaps help him if he remembers that by his own act he is now in worse case than were the original disciples before the resurrection. According to Luke at least they had Jesus' special powers to attract them (5:1–11).[6] In spite of his disability, it is necessary for the inquirer still to ask himself, as Jesus' contemporaries did, "What manner of man is this? Whose son is he?"

They, of course, affirm that they had many later experiences of him in the course of his ministry which convinced them that he was no ordinary man. No doubt the way in which they record those experiences is coloured by what they came to believe of him after the resurrection event, but that is no reason why we should dismiss them without the most careful investigation. It may be that some of them at least will be found sufficiently factual to leave on us the same impression as they evidently made upon the first disciples. If we can thus establish the facts, we may then go on to consider the interpretation.

On this hypothesis, the question will be whether the interpretation given by Jesus' followers, which ultimately found its way into our New Testament, is the right one. Certainly the question is a little complicated by the fact that there are several different portraits of Jesus even in the New Testament. But the differences are mostly in details; and it is really quite evident what type of person all these writers alike thought Jesus to be. He was above everything the person who came to save his people from their sins.

We must remember further that Paul began writing within a couple of decades after Jesus' death and that the tradition about the true character of the Prophet of Nazareth must have hardened well before Paul began to write. He, on his own evidence, handed on only what he had received. This implies that by the time of his conversion there was already a hard core of both fact and interpretation which was accepted and proclaimed by the apostolic leaders and by the general run of the 'faithful'.

The fact that Paul was compelled by the force of his own genius to submit what he had received to consideration in the light of the Hellenistic culture in the midst of which he had been nurtured, and that he was led to blaze the trail towards an ultimate systematisation in the light of contemporary knowledge, certainly does not suggest that the hard core was not there already, or that Paul was led to invent the essential elements of Christian faith. On the contrary it is hard to conceive how the apostle could have built up such meagre elements of a system as are acknowledged even by those scholars who accept only a bare minimum of the Pauline corpus as authentic, if he had not had a solid foundation on which to begin his construction.

As we have already seen, a few modern scholars have tried to turn his declaration of a readiness to forgo his knowledge of Christ 'in the flesh' (2 Cor. 5 : 16) into an assertion that he was not interested in the 'quest of the historical Jesus'. But that is a piece of bad exegesis. What St. Paul meant was that one must not stop at a mere knowledge of the earthly life and career of Jesus, but must go on to know him in his eternal character, by which he is available to his worshippers throughout the ages, not as a mere figure of past history but here and now. That surely is a profound truth of the spiritual life. Later it was to be expressed in Colossians as the identification of the historic Jesus with the pre-existent and eternal Christ.

No doubt as soon as contemporaries departed from the known facts there would begin a temptation to ask oneself what 'must have happened'. And the stronger one's belief in the divine nature of the Christ the more easily one would be inclined to imagine the sort of historical situation that 'must' have arisen to display that nature. Without question a proportion even of the synoptic story may have arisen under that kind of pressure. It is probably in this region that what we have said above about such things as myth, legend and symbol can most readily be applied. We may legitimately wonder for instance how much or how little the birth tradition, as given in Matthew and Luke, owes to this kind of influence.

Scholars will continue to differ about which elements in the story are strictly factual and which are the precipitate of pious imagination. The New Testament writers do not seem to have greatly worried about historical precision except in respect to the most fundamental facts. At any rate, they are always ready to improve on one another, as St. Luke's prologue frankly acknowledges. Nevertheless it is hypercriticism to say that the sole reliable facts are that Jesus actually lived and really died.

It is very doubtful whether the primitive Christian Church would have survived at all, much less made its rapid expansion, if its original members had believed no more than that. In fact everyone admits the tremendous effect on them of their belief that Jesus had risen from the dead and had been actually seen alive. One can well imagine the kind of effect such a belief must have had on those who held it. A proportion of modern scholars is prepared to leave the question there, and not to probe any further into the validity of such a belief. It can safely be assumed, however, that the general conscience of Christendom could never be content to leave the very foundation of its religion thus dangling in the air. If the resurrection of Jesus is the cornerstone of the whole structure of faith, we must know both what the belief involves and whether it is valid.

According to von Campenhausen (*Tradition and Life*, p. 84) "the decisive impulse that set everything in motion was the discovery of the empty tomb". To this all the evangelists bear witness. Their unanimity suggests that it formed part of the basic Christian tradition. There is really nothing in the documents against this. All the strictly historical evidence we have is in favour of it, and those scholars who reject it ought to recognise that they do so on some other ground than that of scientific history.

The situation is not so easy when we come to inquire the *reason* for the tomb's emptiness. As is well known, the New Testament itself records different reasons. According to Matthew the soldiers on guard were bribed to say that Jesus' disciples had stolen the body, but the four evangelists agree in maintaining that the reason for the emptiness was that Jesus had risen bodily from the dead. A couple of decades and more before the evangelists published their gospels Paul had endorsed this interpretation, though without explicit reference to the empty tomb. He believed wholeheartedly in the resurrection *on the third day* (1 Cor. 15:4), and this appears to imply the empty tomb. But he preferred to rest his judgment on the explicit evidence of Christ's appearance to himself, and upon a comprehensive list of appearances to others which seems independent of the tradition used by the evangelists.

Of the total effect of the belief in these appearances there can be no doubt. They led to a reappraisal of the person of Jesus, to the Christian mission, to the founding of the Church, and to the selection of a definite body of people who had 'seen the Lord' to act as witnesses and ministers. While all of them probably regarded the appearances of the 'risen' Jesus as the authority for their personal claims, they would obviously have found themselves in an equivocal position, if it could have been proved (as their opponents were most anxious to prove) that the tomb had never been found empty. Here, as so often in the New Testament, fact and explanation go together. It was not that someone was first persuaded of the resurrection and then supported it by the story of the empty tomb, but the tomb was first found empty and then immediately the explanation was found in the resurrection.

It remains true, however, that quite a number of scholars who are ready to talk of the 'resurrection event' are not willing to accept the historicity of the empty tomb. Somewhat paradoxically they accept the explanation (even if only in a 'spiritual' form) without accepting the fact. Would it be possible on a wider front to turn the paradox inside out? Are there any aspects of the life of Jesus where we can find a general acceptance of the facts irrespective of the interpretation?

One thinks of the general outline of the life as given by the synoptists. It is true that, since the emergence of form criticism, we have accepted the view that no reliance can be placed on the order in which the fragments of tradition have been pieced together in the gospels. Mark seems to have tried to pursue a roughly chronological order, while Matthew has arranged the pieces according to subjects, and Luke may have taken locality as the keynote of his arrangement. Nevertheless it does so happen that the general outline of the narrative follows a common chronological line of considerable verisimilitude. In the story of the ministry there is first a period of mounting popularity. This culminates in the confession of St. Peter that Jesus is the Messiah, followed by the transfiguration. After this peak point there is a gradual deterioration of Jesus' relations with authority, leading to his passion and ultimate death and rising again.

This outline seems to represent the convergence of a number of traditions. It contains many arguable episodes including the problematic transfiguration, to say nothing of the triumphant culmination in the resurrection. But as descriptive of a mere popular movement, first up and then down, it seems likely enough. It is indeed all the more likely for not having been obviously contrived. May not the historian be on fairly safe technical ground in accepting it?

If this is so, then we are getting much nearer to a historical foundation for the life of Christ than seemed at one time possible. True, this is merely framework, but every detail of the picture itself is subject to examination. The method of such examination will presently be described below (see ch. 10). Much scholarly work has accumulated during the last generation, far too much to be discussed here and now. It must be granted that the results are thoroughly diverse: some incidents are accepted as having at least a high degree of probability; others are rejected as being improbable in themselves and resting upon insufficient evidence; while an intermediate selection are seen to be acceptable only when purified from some elements of myth, legend, or symbol.

However many stories have thus to be pruned down or dropped altogether, there is surely enough narrative material left to give us a trustworthy picture of the Prophet of Nazareth. It is true that we may lose the clear-line portraits of the past: the simple moralist who proclaimed love to God and one's neighbour, the stained-glass figure compounded of traditional dogma and romantic idealism, the political reformer who was more than half a revolutionary, the apocalyptic fanatic who expected the world to end its material existence with his own death. All these and many more may be found to be much too positive and clear cut. But enough remains to give us a picture of a prophetic teacher of humble birth who had a remarkably independent method of handling the religion of his nation, a moralist who could speak fearlessly to the leaders of his people and gently to children and old people, a healer who left a strong record of success particularly with what we should call nervous or mental cases, a leader who himself bore hardship calmly and refused to avoid the possibility of an agonising death, and who, if he has become known as 'the man for others', was above all the man for God.

When we have assimilated these basic elements in the New Testament picture of Jesus we can turn back to the one-sided portraits we have just dismissed and recognise that each one of them contains some element of verisimilitude, some recognisable feature. We can then proceed to build up our own composite portrait of Jesus, which, however wide it may be of the mark, is still far better than the 'identikit' which is often the only guide the detective may have to the appearance of his criminal.

To this partial knowledge we have to add all that can be gleaned of the character of Jesus from his reported teaching. As we have seen, the present tendency is to regard this material as on the whole more reliable than the strictly narrative portion of the evidence. It is certainly true that a good deal may be learned about the character of a man from the quality of his teaching. What we can learn in this way can assuredly add a good deal of colour to the portrait we already have of Jesus.

Altogether we can safely say that much too much has been made of the difficulty of forming a picture of Jesus that will satisfy the demands of history. It is certain that we can never be sure that we have a precisely accurate picture. But then one can never be certain of that even in the case of a contemporary still alive. How seldom is a painting taken as 'a good likeness' by the sitter's relatives and friends! A long-suffering artist once defined a portrait as 'a picture of a person with something wrong about the mouth'. It should put no great strain on our conscience as historians, if we were a little more ready to be satisfied with what we have in the way of evidence than many of us actually are.[7] Indeed we might be inclined to be more suspicious, if our information were more precise and detailed. After all, we are dealing with the first century and not the twentieth. It would be thoroughly un-historical and indeed anachronistic to judge the methods of the evangelists by our own. Nevertheless we are conscious of receiving from the New Testament a fundamentally consistent portrait of an easily identifiable person. If we could not write a biographical 'life' of Jesus, we could at any rate give a reliable picture of him which everyone would recognise. And this is based mainly on the factual or narrative evidence.

The story is somewhat more complicated when in seeking an answer to the question, "Who art thou, Lord?", we come to consider the *interpretation* of the facts. Is there any compelling reason to think that we have here the portrait of anyone other than a mere man?

Notes

[1] Kegan Paul (1935), pp. 537, 538.
[2] Hodder and Stoughton (1935).
[3] See Wand, *Transfiguration* (Faith Press, 1967).
[4] *Life of Jesus* (Allen and Unwin, 1933), pp. 60, 201.
[5] Barth's commentary was first published in English in 1933 (O.U.P.).

[6] It should be noted, however, that Mark (1: 16–20) and Matthew (4: 18–22) are silent about the draught of fishes and its evidential value.

[7] A much more detailed and 'sceptical' approach to this problem may be studied in F. G. Downing, *The Church and Jesus* (S.C.M., 1968).

8

Son of Man and Lord

Before we answer that question, we ought to make up our mind on the one fundamental point: are we prepared to rule out from the beginning all intervention of a 'supernatural' in the natural sphere? That would be a much more tempting way of escape for the historian than is often realised by traditionalist thinkers.

Under modern terms he is precluded from bringing in the supernatural to explain anything unusual in the situations with which he deals. His natural tendency is to polish away the novel and the mysterious as roughnesses which must be eliminated. His business is to show cause and effect running smoothly on the assembly line of space and time. He is uncomfortable in the presence of the apparently unique. When faced by some suggestion of God's activity in the universe, it is easy for him to say with a deprecatory shrug, "I have no need of that hypothesis."

A more subtle temptation is faced by the 'secular' theologian of the type who insists on the existence of God only so long as he is not pictured as taking any distinctive part in the world's affairs or, which amounts to the same thing, only so long as he is so closely identified with the process of causation that his distinctive personal presence is not discernible.

Both types of thought are common enough in these days. If we yield to either of them it is clear that we can give no unbiassed opinion on the main question at issue. We shall be bound to regard Jesus as a common member of the human race with, no doubt, a certain outstanding genius as thinker and leader, but certainly with no claim to be regarded as of a different genus from ordinary men.

In other words it is only as we are prepared to regard an incarnation or a special revelation as a possibility that it is worth while considering the question at all. If we are not, then it is obvious that we have already returned a negative answer to the question and that to pursue it would be a waste of time. It is to be feared that quite a number of scholars have accepted this alternative without stating their presuppositions even to themselves. They have thought that they were coming to the question with an open mind, when in point of fact they regard it as nonsensical from the outset.

On the other hand there are millions of people who are already believers in some sort of revelation and even incarnation who are still unwilling to think of Jesus as more than a human figure. They would accept a residuum of the historic facts as outlined, even perhaps some of the miracles, but would not necessarily regard Jesus as therefore divine. It is those only who have an open mind at least to this extent who are likely to be interested in further discussion.

Let us remind ourselves once more how far history has been able to take us (or most of us). We know that Jesus was a Jewish prophet belonging to early first-century Palestine, that he was born of humble parentage, and was somehow mixed up in the reformation of Judaism attempted by John the Baptist, whose preaching work he took over together with his initiation ceremony of baptism. After a very short period of one to three years, during which he gained a considerable reputation as a healer and a story-teller, he ran foul of both the ecclesiastical and military authorities and was executed by crucifixion. What he left behind was no sacred book or building but a small body of disciples who, after a moment of panic, persuaded themselves that he had risen again from the dead. On that basis there developed an organisation which at first included only a handful of Jews, then began to spread among the people of other races (mostly Jewish proselytes) in Palestine, and presently became an international organisation recognisable as the Church.

What is remarkable about this story is the effect made upon his contemporaries by the personality of Jesus. Both professional theologians and ordinary Bible-reading Christians are so familiar with the narratives of the gospels that it is difficult for them to appreciate the startling force of this impact. It is only when some fresh shock, or sudden access of insight, stabs us broad awake that we see for ourselves the startling fascination exercised by this traditional figure as depicted in the gospels.

A good impression of this kind of effect can be gained from the work of a non-theologian who after long familiarity with the classics was set to translate the gospels afresh for a popular clientèle. The introduction written by E. V. Rieu for his Penguin translation of the four gospels brings out clearly the dominant influence of the personality of Jesus. Rieu is seeking an explanation why, with everything against them, the evangelists were able to produce such a masterpiece, unique in the history of literature and in the annals of religion. "We can account for it only by remembering that they were inspired by a unique personality. Just as Jesus lived in the oral tradition that preceded the gospels, so he inspired and unified the writings that eventually summed it up. One might almost say that Jesus wrote the gospels."

To this statement we must add the undoubted fact that the personality of Jesus still has the same kind of effect on millions of people, who derive their first impression of him either from the teaching of Christian believers or from their own reading of the New Testament. This is not the kind of evidence that can be weighed in the balances of critical inquiry, but it is nevertheless a stupendous fact, which it would be highly unscientific to ignore. Through two thousand years of history and much re-translating the person of Jesus as depicted in the gospels still presents men with a challenge they may accept or refuse but cannot ignore.

All this, we can fairly claim, should be taken into consideration in any effort to frame a genuinely historical picture of Jesus. It is a good deal more than the mere data of existence and violent death which is all that some historians in their more pessimistic moments are inclined to allow as the result of scientific investigation. It is probable, however, that a considerable proportion of what has been said above would be readily admitted by the vast majority of competent historians. If now we can regard these as the 'agreed facts' of history, we have to go on to the much more difficult question of the interpretation of these facts. How does the view of Jesus taken in the New Testament and in later generations square with these basic facts?

Käsemann asks whether it is possible to show an identity

between Jesus the preacher and the Jesus who was the (later) object of preaching. He picks out four particular points at which there seems a clear connection between the Jesus of history and the Christ of the early Church: Jesus' message of a gracious God, his independent criticism of the Mosaic law, his demand for obedience and love towards himself, and his death as a logical culmination of his ministry. Käsemann describes these as "decisive pivotal points which allow continuity to be established"[1] They all alike appear in the authentic gospel narrative and they are basic to the *Kerygma*.

We should be greatly helped in our efforts to answer this question more fully if we knew precisely what Jesus thought of himself. That is not at all easy to find out. We know roughly what the evangelists thought that he thought of himself, for they may seem to have no hesitation in making him utter what they considered to be the appropriate sentiments about himself. It was the common method of the time for a writer so to express the character of his hero. In the days when there were no tape-recorders and no very adequate shorthand system it is doubtful whether any other method was even possible, although a good deal must be allowed for unspoilt memories of a powerful speaker.

It has consequently become one of the most delicate exercises of New Testament criticism to disentangle the various versions of what Jesus is alleged to have said about himself. Joachim Jeremias[2] thinks that in the account of the Last Supper he can get back to the Aramaic phrases actually used by Jesus over the bread and the wine. An instance in which Jesus' Aramaic words do seem to have been precisely preserved is the cry from the cross (Mark 15:34). But whether Jeremias thinks we may count the phrase *'Talitha cumi'*, used

at the raising of the damsel (Mark 5:41), as equally indica-
tive of authenticity does not appear.

The title Jesus seems to have used most frequently of himself is 'Son of Man'. It has long been suggested that this
title includes two strongly contrasted ideas, first that of
humiliation closely associated with, if not dependent upon,
the picture of the Suffering Servant of God in Isaiah 53, and,
second, that of an apocalyptic descent in glory on the clouds
of heaven at the end of time as judge of the world and saviour
of mankind. A third suggestion is that it means simply the
first person singular, the pronoun I.

In a comparatively recent study,[3] F. H. Borsch has tried
to show that the phrase means the quintessential man, or the
royal man, and goes back into pre-history when the leader
was bound up in the well-being of his people and was expected to suffer and, if need be, die on their behalf. This
idea, says Borsch, lasted into the period of the Hebrew mon-
archy and led to the king being regarded as in some sense
divine, embodying in himself the archetypal image of his
people. The essential unity of God, Son of Man and people
was symbolised, says Borsch, in coronation and baptismal
rites. It was this essential unity that Jesus meant to embody
in the title Son of Man as applied to himself. But when they
saw the age-long conception fulfilled in their contemporary,
his followers preserved the living reality they found in him
and let the archaic ideas behind it fall into desuetude. Consequently in the early Church the Son of Man title was allowed
to drop. In this case at least myth would thus have been
replaced by history.

A good deal of such learned elaboration may be regarded
as fanciful, but it is a fair example of the interest aroused

among scholars by the title Son of Man. They generally recognise that it is full of meaning and must have had for contemporaries many overtones which are difficult for us to capture. Not many run to the other extreme and accept the jejune interpretation which makes the phrase mean no more than 'I', a particular example of man in general. Most agree that it contains the double idea of humility and exaltation, and a considerable proportion would see in it a hidden suggestion of Messiahship. In any case it appears to have been Jesus' specific name for himself.[4] If it does not disclose for us any precise indication of his thoughts concerning his own function and character, it does at least suggest that he felt himself to be a man of destiny, a particular kind of person with a particular mission to fulfil. And this is sufficiently obvious to the average reader from the general tone of all the gospels, quite apart from any specific claim.

There are, of course, in our present gospels many passages in which Jesus claims for himself a position far more than human. The fourth gospel is so full of such sentiments that they are regarded as characteristically 'Johannine' and are consequently much discounted. But some doubt is cast upon this quick and easy method of exegesis by the recollection of a very Johannine passage in St. Luke (10:17–24). It was after the return of the Seventy with their news of a mission successfully accomplished. Jesus was so moved as to say that he saw Satan falling like lightning from heaven, and he goes on, "All things have been delivered unto me of my Father; and no one knoweth who the Son is save the Father, and who the Father is, save the Son and he to whomsoever the Son willeth to reveal him."

These are hardly the words of a normal person who

regards himself as no different from other men. If we accept them as the actual words of Jesus (and we must remember that St. Matthew also repeats them, 11:25–30),[5] then we must agree that Jesus thus early in his ministry did see himself as someone set apart from the rest of mankind.

It is impossible for us here to linger over details of what Jesus may have been held to have spoken of himself. Each of such detailed expressions is the subject of much scholarly discussion. It is better for us to try to seize the general atmosphere, relying upon those elements on which there is fairly general agreement. The title Son of Man is widely accepted as at least implying something special, and is all the more conspicuous because it is so seldom employed by anyone other than Jesus himself. The passage about the mutual knowledge of the Father and the Son is almost equally conspicuous because (in spite of the birth narratives) it is so unexpected in the synoptic tradition.

We can pass on then to ask how the early disciples of Jesus interpreted the facts they knew about the Master. Here we are fortunate in that St. Paul was writing well before the synoptic tradition had taken shape. We notice that already he had a favourite title for Jesus, that of *Kyrios* or Lord. Unfortunately, perhaps, this is another title with a vast range of possible meanings. In classical circles it might mean anything from Mister to the Emperor, *dominus ac noster deus*. What was more important, in Jewish circles it might go further still and imply the greatest of all dignities. The Septuagint used it as a translation of the name Jehovah, Jahweh, the sole and absolute God, whose proper name was so exalted that it must never be pronounced.

In view of the possible connotation of the term, one would expect Paul to be extremely cautious in his use of it. On the contrary, he employs it as descriptive of Jesus with the utmost freedom and never seems afraid of any possible exaggeration. Yet his whole Jewish instinct must have made him recoil against the impropriety of using for a man a title that might be regarded as specially applicable to the godhead. The extraordinary thing is that Paul comes before us so soon with so highly developed a Christology. One would not have thought that sufficient time had elapsed for such a development, unless a vigorous impulse had already been given in the self-disclosure of the Master.

Paul came to the situation with a fresh mind. He had known about Jesus only from the point of view of an avowed enemy and a recognised persecutor. Then quite suddenly he had been caught by the post-resurrection faith in Jesus, evinced by the people he was hunting to death. This faith, which he found confirmed in his own experience, he had the opportunity of thinking out for himself during his years of retreat. He further had a valuable opportunity of testing it out in his preaching and teaching after he had been accepted as an active collaborator with the disciples in the missionary task of the Church. And then he began setting it forth, not systematically, but at least reasonably and logically, in written answers to questions and in written judgments on problems and situations as they arose. The result is admittedly a somewhat casual collection of foundation principles, but in his essential attitude to the person of Christ Paul is hardly likely to have differed seriously from his colleagues who were in the faith before him.

True, it is sometimes suggested that this witness of St.

Paul is weakened by the fact that modern scholarship has cast doubts on the authorship of some of the letters attributed to him. It has long been recognised that the Epistle to the Hebrews must have come from another hand, although the position adopted in that letter can be described as roughly Pauline, and the author, whoever it was, must have belonged to a school strongly influenced by Paul. But for the rest the letters, where they are not all accepted as in some degree authentic, are generally divided into three groups, the genuinely Pauline (Thessalonians, Galatians, Corinthians, Romans), the possibly Pauline (Colossians, Ephesians, Philemon, Philippians); and the post-Pauline (Timothy and Titus). It is pointed out that the most exalted teaching about Jesus as the Christ is to be found in the middle group. There he is depicted as the agent in creation, an eternal and universal personality, the head of the Church, the goal of all history.

Probably no one since Paul Sabatier has wished to deny that there was any development in Paul's thought (he would have been a singular person if there was not), but this is very far from suggesting that between the two first groups of letters there is a jump from a purely humanistic interpretation of the Person of Christ to a fully Catholic Christology. Already in the earlier group Jesus is the Lord who will come again in glory at the second advent; he is the redeemer whose self-sacrifice has won our salvation, and faith in whom ensures our freedom; he is the Messiah in whose name believers are baptised, the one foundation upon which all must build. But why go on? To the candid reader it should be obvious that from the beginning of his writing St. Paul looks upon Jesus as a very special messenger from God, related to him not only by ties of discipleship but by those of most intimate kinship. In this respect at least there is no break or illogical step between the various groups of the Pauline epistles.

It is admitted that the term 'kinship' is somewhat unusual in this connection, but it is difficult to find another which would adequately express Paul's obvious feelings about the relation between the persons in the Trinity, which he in some sense already recognises. "The grace of our Lord Jesus Christ and the love of God and the fellowship of the Holy Ghost" (2 Cor. 13:14). One does not suggest that St. Paul had reached the point arrived at later by the Council of Nicea in A.D. 325 when it defined the relation of Jesus to the Father as *homoousios* (of one substance). It still required a good deal more thinking in a more Hellenic atmosphere before that solution could be reached. But at least we can say that Paul was already on the way there, and that the definition when it was achieved, was in harmony with his thought.

There is really then no doubt how the apostle interpreted the facts about Jesus. However meticulous we may be about the niceties of the terms in which he expressed his thought, he had certainly reached the conclusion that Jesus Christ was more than ordinary man, that he existed before the created world and would continue to exist after it, that he was in a particular sense God's Son incarnate as Jesus of Nazareth, destined to be the moral and spiritual saviour of the world.

It can hardly be doubted that this is the view taken also by the evangelists. The synoptists do not express it so openly as the writer of the fourth gospel, who may indeed be

110

thought to carry it a stage further by associating it so definitely with the doctrine of the Logos; but even that is very much in line with their 'post-resurrection' estimate of Jesus, an estimate which, as we have seen, inevitably coloured to some extent their narrative.

It would be a mistake, however, to see in this development nothing more than the influence of Paul. The time is long past when a scholar like Pfleiderer could see in Paul the sole source of the Christological doctrine of the New Testament. We have become aware in more recent years of a number of different approaches to Christology in the canon of sacred writings. These differing views undoubtedly go back to different traditions. Just as the evangelists drew upon different collections of stories, whether written or oral, to compile their narratives, so other New Testament writers drew upon various interpretations of Jesus' teaching. Even Paul himself, who seems proud of his own independent thinking does not seek to disguise the fact that there was much that he had 'received' not only by revelation but by tradition.[6]

From our present point of view the interesting thing is that the various interpretations are so strikingly similar. There are indeed differences in the method of approach, but the result is the same. Whether we are dealing with the Pauline, the Petrine, or the Johannine letters it is essentially the same Christ we are invited to meet. That is also true of the Epistle to the Hebrews. A possible exception must be made in the case of the Epistle of James, but it is difficult to judge because in that epistle Christology is reduced to a minimum. In that respect it may be said to approximate more nearly to the teaching of Jesus, who talked more about his

Father than about himself. It probably reflects the views of a Jewish Christian section of the Church; and it is quite possible that it did not go much beyond accepting Jesus as Messiah, although that was already setting him on a pinnacle above ordinary men.

We do know that there was a sect of Ebionites, regarded as heretical, who took a deliberately minimising view of the person of Jesus, reducing him to the stature of a mere man. It is sometimes thought that there may have been some association between such people and at least a section of the Jewish Christians. There is, however, no certainty on this matter, and it does not seem likely that Paul would have had many dealings with James or anyone else if he thought that they denied the divinity of Christ.

The difference or suspected difference between Paul and James on the subject of faith is well known. It would hardly be fair to argue from that difference to a conflict in Christology. Certainly Paul appears to think that essential Christianity means incorporation into Christ (Rom. 6:5 *N.E.B.*). If that mystical type of thought is alien to the mind of James, he nevertheless seems to approximate closely to the thought of Paul when he speaks of the Judge at the door and uses the term Lord in such a way as to make it necessary to decide whether he is applying it to Jehovah or to Jesus (2:1, 5:8–11).

In the present position of research most scholars would agree that, apart from niceties of detail, the New Testament writers are united in recognising Jesus as more than ordinary man and as at least approximating to the general idea of deity. This view comes out with special emphasis in such historical passages as those narrating the baptism of Jesus,

the declaration of Peter at Caesarea Philippi, the transfiguration, the voice from heaven after the interview with the
Greeks, the resurrection. How much of these narratives is
mere report of factual tradition and how much is due to the
accumulation of interpretation in the course of transmission
we may never be able to decide. What we cannot avoid trying
to decide is whether the interpretation is on the whole
reliable or not.

Notes

[1] Ernst Käsemann, *New Testament Questions of Today*
(S.C.M., 1969), p. 64.

[2] *The Eucharistic Words of Jesus* (S.C.M., 1966), p. 220.

[3] *The Son of Man in Myth and History* (S.C.M., 1967), *passim*.

[4] Needless to say, this is disputed by some, like everything else
in this sphere.

[5] If this means that the passage comes from Q, then we have
another written tradition betraying the standpoint of John.

[6] See 1 Cor. 11: 23, 15: 3; Gal. 1: 12; 2 Thess. 3: 6.

9

Kerygma and Fact

The outstanding announcement of the New Testament as a whole is that of Jesus' resurrection. This appeared to contemporary disciples to carry with it convincing proof of his Messiahship and to point in the direction of what we now call the incarnation. Naturally enough, neither of these points was very precisely defined. Centuries of faith and debate were to contribute to the logical refining of their implications. They were neither of them mere statements of fact. They were conclusions derived in large measure from an accepted fact, the resurrection event, the discovery that Jesus' tomb was empty and that he had appeared on a number of occasions after his death to various disciples.

Rénan reduced the evidence for this alleged fact to the outcry of one hysterical woman. Whether Paul would have agreed with that estimate in the days before his conversion we have no means of knowing. We have every reason to think that after his conversion he accepted the reality of the resurrection as other Christians did. He had the more reason to believe it, not merely because he knew a number of instances in which Jesus had been seen after his resurrection, but because he was convinced that he had actually seen him himself.

This argument is not likely to be as convincing to us as it

was to St. Paul. He does not draw the sharp distinction, which is common to us, between the physical and the psychical. He equates the appearance of Jesus to himself with the appearances to the 'witnesses of the resurrection' ("Am I not an apostle? have I not seen the Lord?" 1 Cor. 9:5). But in their case we are expected to regard the appearance as in some sense physical, while in his case, whatever St. Paul may have thought himself, we are much more likely to assume that it was psychological. It is possible, of course, that the evangelists felt this kind of difficulty about the difference between physical and psychological and tried to meet it with the implied suggestion of a 'spiritual' or 'heavenly' body, which could appear in a closed room and was capable of levitation, a suggestion that is found in St. Paul's own discussion of the Christian's resurrection body (1 Cor. 15:51 ff). But the only hint of such a distinction, in the accounts of Paul's conversion, is that his companions did not see the 'vision', which was so vivid a reality to their leader. (See also 1 Cor. 15:8.)

In any case, Paul, after his conversion, found himself a member of a community bound together by their belief in the physical resurrection of Jesus. No doubt the pressure of such an environment, in spite of his natural independence, would help to confirm his acceptance of the teaching of the resurrection. But it cannot be too fully recognised that, so far as our information goes, the belief came to him quite unexpectedly, literally out of the blue.

As for the other New Testament writers, we can recognise that they also found in their conceptual environment influences that would help them to believe in a spiritual role as particularly appropriate to Jesus. We have the background

Platonism of the Epistle to the Hebrews, the Logos mysticism of the fourth gospel, the Old Testament Messianism of St. James, the continued prophetism of 1 Peter. All these influences, like the Pharisaism of St. Paul, might help to foster a belief in the resurrection.

But it is extremely unlikely, in spite of what one knows or guesses about the incipient Gnosticism of the period, that any process of spontaneous generation could have given rise to the specific belief in the resurrection of Jesus, unless there had been some such physical fact as the empty tomb to act as the first creative impulse. It was the fact that drove the believers to find an explanation, not the explanation that demanded some fact to give it foundation. The empty tomb was an accepted fact of the tradition. Alternative explanations of it were possible. Resurrection was the one that commended itself to contemporaries, and was confirmed by the appearances. Some accepted it, and did not shrink from the inevitable corollary, a belief in the special relation of Jesus to God. It was from that point of view that the evangelists ultimately told the story of Jesus' life and teaching.

They had a good deal of varied material to work upon, and they did not all write with precisely the same purpose in mind. The fourth gospel is the most explicit as to its intentions: "These things are written, that you may believe that Jesus is the Christ, the Son of God; and that believing you may have life in his name" (John 20:31). In other words it was a piece of deliberate and open propaganda intended to support the Christian mission. The very prologue seeks to establish the identity of the historic Jesus of Nazareth with the eternal Word or Reason of God.

The writer of the third gospel is almost as explicit and

even more informative as to his method. He is writing for a distinguished patron and tells him "I have decided to write a connected narrative for you, so as to give you authentic and ordered knowledge about the matters of which you have been informed" (Luke 1:3, 4). He is evidently concerned about the somewhat chaotic state into which the information about Jesus has fallen and he wants to straighten it out for a man of some position and intelligence. What he has to work upon is a number of documents purporting to give an account of comparatively recent events. They did not spring out of nothing but were themselves based, to some extent, on other documents and to some extent on eyewitness reports.

We are morally certain that one of those available documents was that which we know as the Gospel according to Mark, of which Luke appears to borrow about 330 verses. An interesting point, which shows that the first gospel also reveals the same sort of method in its composition, is that Matthew uses much more of Mark, roughly about 590 verses. There is also another block of material common to both Matthew and Luke, but not to be found in Mark at all, consisting of rather more than 200 verses. This situation has led to the theory that both authors used a second document besides Mark. This theory has been much blown upon of late and it is sometimes objected that this second document, known as Q (*quelle* or source), never existed. But it cannot be said that the objection has been fully sustained. Indeed there are recently discovered documents, such as the Gnostic *Gospel of Thomas*, which belong precisely to the type that might have included Q, that is to say, they are almost entirely concerned with the teaching of Jesus to the exclusion of his acts.

117

In addition to Mark and Q, Luke evidently had a source of his own, from which he drew about 400 verses for the general course of his narrative, and another from which he drew 130 or so verses describing the incidents connected with the birth of Jesus. This makes four documents in all for Luke. Arguing along the same lines New Testament scholars are generally agreed that Matthew also had four documents to draw upon: Mark, Q, a source (about 230 verses) peculiar to himself and an Antiochene version of the birth stories, which of course is quite different from Luke's.

But all this is *vieux jeu*. In recent years scholars have been trying with renewed vigour to get behind these documents to the oral traditions that must have formed their basis. It has been found comparatively easy to analyse the documents into their component parts, such as could easily have been learned by heart or become stereotyped in the reiterated lessons of teachers. The story of the woman taken in adultery is already shown by its varying position in the Greek text to be separable. It is a matter of common knowledge that many other incidents, when they are shared by two or more of the evangelists, do not occupy the same position in the general course of the narrative. The conclusion is inevitable that the gospels, as we have them, are collections of discrete traditions.

It may well have been the evangelists who imposed order upon them. St. Luke told his patron (1:4) expressly that it was part of his object to write a *connected* narrative for him. But on what system the connection was made he does not tell. It may have been chronological, it may have been in accordance with subject matter, or even by locality, as we have earlier suggested. In any case the many fragments of tradition must have presented the writers with a tremendous jigsaw puzzle, and its solving was obviously done at more than one stage. Even so the evangelists found plenty of scope for their own individuality, and by no means always reached the same conclusions.

The effect of these inquiries upon the effort to form a historically reliable portrait of Jesus has been mentioned. They have put an end, for the time being at least, to the belief that one can write a chronologically accurate biography.[1] They have also cast fresh doubt on the credibility of various parts of the story. It has been noted that some of the fragments, the miracle stories, for example, often follow lines that are common to contemporary pagan or hellenistic stories of a similar type. The looking up to heaven, the sighing or sufflation, the use of spittle, the touching, can all be paralleled from contemporary pagan and Jewish sources. If the mechanism is the same, can we justly give credence to the biblical narrative while refusing it to the others?

Such doubts may seem a heavy price to pay to form criticism for the undoubted advantage it has given us in getting a step nearer to the original narrators of stories about Jesus. Many English scholars at least are prepared to pursue that advantage to the utmost, while refusing to accept the derogatory judgment derived by some critics from the similarity between the 'forms' of biblical and non-biblical narratives.

At present more interest is being shown in the light thrown on the evangelists' method of interpretation and so on their theology. The advance made in analysis of the documents has made possible a further step in the disentanglement of the thoughts of the original narrator from those of the evangelist

119

who records his story and combines it with others to make a continuous theme. The method known as 'redaction' criticism consists in an effort to distinguish between the story itself, which may be assumed to be the original narrator's, and the framework in which it is set, which may be assumed to be the evangelist's. As has already been mentioned, the situation may be most clearly seen in the case of some of the parables, where the framework seems to suggest a point or 'moral' of the story which sometimes differs from that of the narrator. But the same principle may be seen at work in some accounts of miracles and controversies.

This method of using a report or a record as an opportunity of teaching doctrine is found at its most obvious in the fourth gospel. Take for instance the famous sixth chapter in which the feeding of the 'great multitude' becomes the basis of an exposition first of the Bread of Life and then of the Eucharist. Again the story of the healing of the man blind from birth (9:1-40) becomes, naturally enough, a simile of spiritual enlightenment and so of the inevitable 'judgment' that Jesus' coming must involve for the world. In some instances, of course, it is more than possible that Jesus himself drew the required lesson, but it is more commonly considered that, since the style of both narrative and teaching seem peculiar to John, the moral also should be attributed to him.

Recently scholars have been finding instances of the same procedure (the adding of a framework to an original narrative) in the synoptic gospels, particularly St. Luke. It is important for its effect on exegesis. Whereas, for instance, one distinguished commentator, ignoring the suggestion of a framework, sees the main point of the story of the miraculous draught of fishes as Jesus' desire to 'bring fresh courage to dispirited workmen', others see in it Luke's determined effort to keep alive the sense of mission in the Church of his own generation. This interpretation he emphasises in the final exhortation: "Fear not, from henceforth thou shalt catch men" (Luke 5:10).

St. Luke has been carefully examined from this particular angle by Helmut Flender, whose conclusions are sufficiently indicated in the title of his book *St. Luke—Theologian of Redemptive History*.[2] The same service has been performed for St. Matthew by J. D. Kingsbury in *The Parables of Jesus in Matthew 13*.[3] The latter allots the same kind of role to his author, acclaiming 'Matthew' as a theologian who uses the scant framework in which he sets Jesus' stories as an opportunity to give his own particular twist to the moral of the tale and applying it to the needs of his contemporary readers.

An interesting example of the method is to be seen in Kingsbury's handling of Matthew's introduction to his chapter of parables (13:1–3a). Twice, says Kingsbury, Matthew refers to Jesus' sitting (a posture of dignity) while the crowd stands. "It would seem, then, that Matthew's intention in v. 2 is to fashion a setting that will in itself attribute honour to Jesus and underline, not merely a Rabbinic but even a divine dignity." (Cf. the apocalyptic picture of God sitting on his throne while a great crowd of worshippers, men and angels stand before him, in Rev. 7:9–12.) Of course it may be objected that things could just have happened that way. But, if so, why does Matthew, alone of the synoptists, make the point about the contrast between the 'sitting' of Jesus and the standing of the people?

From our present point of view the interesting fact is that, in spite of possible differences as to content and even meaning of the parable, there appears to be no vital difference between the evangelist's estimate of Jesus and that of the original narrator or of the tradition from which Matthew drew his story; except such development as is naturally attributable to the resurrection. However far we go in the study of our texts, the less likelihood does there appear to be of finding any sudden break between a human Jesus and a divine Christ. If the disciples' recollection of Jesus had been violently different, they would never have been able to identify him with the risen Christ.

That there was an advance during the period of the Lord's ministry, culminating in the recognition of him as Messiah at Caesarea Philippi, is made clear in the gospels themselves. That there was a marked advance in conviction and depth of understanding as a result of the resurrection, culminating in such an outright statement as Thomas's "My Lord and my God", is also part of the gospel story. There is no point at which it can properly be said that the evangelists are doing violence to the evidence they have before them. The Jesus of history is the Christ of the gospel faith.

We may conclude then that the letter-writers and the evangelists of the New Testament are in substantial agreement about their interpretation of the facts of Jesus' life. Whether they are right or wrong in that interpretation is, of course, another matter. It is often alleged that, being children of their time, they were not capable of distinguishing between genuine historical truth and such para-historical material as we have already described in an earlier chapter. Legend, myth, allegory, parable have all been mistaken for history by ancient writers. Is it not possible that the same thing has happened here?

We may say at once that it would have been very odd if nothing at all of the kind had happened. We know in our own experience how stories accumulate around every well-known figure, even during his own lifetime. His 'image' includes some outstanding features, and instances are multiplied to illustrate these well-known characteristics, making them all the more prominent in the process. In this development popular biography follows the art of the caricaturist, which consists in seizing upon some prominent features and exaggerating them so that they later identify the subject in every circumstance and under every disguise.

Jesus seems to have been best known as a healer and a story-teller. No doubt a rich store of anecdotes quickly accumulated in the tradition under both heads. It is surprising how quickly such trivia can be fastened on someone in the public eye.[4] It would be all the easier in contemporary Jewish society since it was the custom of the rabbis to illustrate a point with a *mashal*, which is the nearest equivalent to a parable that ancient literature has to offer. It would be natural to make Jesus the greatest story-teller of them all.

Much the same can be said about the 'signs' or wonders that Jesus is said to have performed. It would be a ridiculous mistake to dismiss them as altogether impossible. A public image does not spring out of nothing. There must be some reason for it, some foundation in fact upon which the popular fancy has built. A feature must be there before it can be exaggerated and caricatured. There can be little doubt, for instance, that Jesus was a successful faith-healer. A knowledge of modern psychology helps us to understand the mechanism by which some of his cures may have been effected. But the attempt to rationalise them out of existence as 'signs and wonders' has always failed. There remains an element of the mysterious about them, while some, like the withering of the barren fig-tree and the emergence of the dead from their graves at the crucifixion, seem, as recorded, inexplicable and even pointless.

The so-called 'nature miracles', which are generally regarded as in a class by themselves, may be viewed either as simple coincidences or as specific manifestations of divine power. The stilling of the storm and the blasting of the fig-tree fall into that alternative. Such an alternative would provide no difficulty for the thorough-going believer in divine providence, who could see the working of God in alleged coincidence just as plainly as in an unusual manifestation of power.

But before ever we spend time over this kind of consideration we ought to make as sure as possible that we really are dealing with what are intended to be plain statements of fact. It is well known that the author of the fourth gospel often describes miracles as *semeia*, signs. As in the case of the feeding of the multitude, he seems more interested in the spiritual implication of the event than in its historical details. We have just suggested that this tendency may be observed, though in a less advanced degree, in the synoptists, especially Luke. It therefore becomes a prior question, in dealing with any miracle, whether the evangelist wishes his story to be taken literally or not. It is always possible that he means the event to be treated as 'acted parable'. That suggestion is often made by commentators to explain the cursing of the barren fig-tree, but it could also be applied to many of the wonder-stories, as for instance the walking on the sea and the stilling of the storm.

How far such a method of exegesis may be justifiably carried is a question demanding careful consideration. It has recently been suggested, for instance, in the press that Luke's versions of the ascension story are intended to be treated in this metaphorical way. The suggestion immediately produced an outcry in humanist quarters that this was a hypocritical effort on the part of Christian teachers to escape from the logical implications of the Bible's explicit statements. Yet the objectors themselves would probably have been the first to repudiate a purely literalistic interpretation in the case of a classical pagan author.

The fact is that we must draw a distinction between a story told for the sake of its moral without any inference as to its factual truth—which makes it a parable—and the drawing of a moral from an event which is accepted as literal occurrence—which makes it history. Luke no doubt fully recognised the moral importance of Christ's triumphal resumption of a life lived in the eternal sphere, but this does not mean that he attached no importance to the appearance of physical levitation in the ascension. Indeed, as the narrative reads, one would have said that Luke drew his conclusion as to the moral situation out of the premises in the physical fact. And that agrees with what we have noticed about his method as revealed in the kind of framework he gave to the traditional narratives in his gospel.

Redaction criticism, or the examination of the individual contribution made by each evangelist in his recording of tradition, shows us how the gospel preaching or *kerygma* was built up. If the *kerygma* is 'the proclamation of the saving acts of God in Christ', the evangelists in narrating the acts bring out their saving qualities. It is not suggested that the evangelists were the initiators of this kind of interpretation. In St. Paul we have it already, in the form in which it is extended to become teaching or *didache*,[5] well before the gospels were published. In this development there must certainly have been a two-way traffic. The *kerygma* helped the evangelists to illuminate the facts while the interpretations of the evangelists reinforced the *kerygma*.

The primitive preachers, like their successors throughout the ages, got their special material where they could find it, but used it only to illustrate or reinforce what had been handed over to them in the tradition. The history in which they were interested was salvation history. It was no less history because they saw in it the hand of God, though it may well be that, being ready to see the hand of God so clearly, they may have imagined wonders where, according to our notions, there were none, or may have exaggerated, as non-scientific witnesses are apt to do, the mysterious or supernatural element in the events they describe. In this process apostles, evangelists, preachers all played their part.

The result is that they certainly did not write what now passes for scientific history. They seem sometimes to have aimed at it when they give us precise information for fixing a date or tracing a pedigree. The mischief is that just when they are trying to be most precise they provide the modern scholar with some of his worst difficulties, as for instance in Luke's dating of the birth and John's of the crucifixion.[6] It becomes clear that their real interest did not lie in this kind of precision but in the great outstanding acts by which God

126

manifested his character and accomplished the salvation of his people.

So we notice in 1 Cor. 15 how St. Paul first reminds the Corinthians of the good news he originally preached to them, which has brought them salvation. He then repeats the twin truths that are the pillars on which the gospel stands—that Jesus died for our sins and that he rose again in accordance with the scriptures. Then he goes on to give precise details to confirm the actual fact of the resurrection. Only after that does he give extended teaching about the nature of the risen life in Christ.

It would thus seem that St. Paul was as aware as we are of the distinctness of the two questions that have been dogging us all the time and which are as relevant in the case of the *kerygma* as in any other section of religion and theology: are the facts as stated well established? and is the part that God is alleged to have played in them secure? Each, as we have realised, needs separate treatment: they do not necessarily stand or fall together.

The difficulty is that so many of the traditionally accepted facts do not now stand out with the clarity and security they once had, though the arguments against them are rather *a priori* than strictly historical. The birth narratives which come from the traditions peculiar to Matthew and Luke respectively are from the documentary point of view some of the least well-attested. What is worse is that they come from an intellectual background in which the appearance of good and bad angels on the stage of space and time was taken very much as a matter of course.

This disability inevitably arouses in one's mind a question as to the authenticity of the event the stories are intended to enshrine, namely the Virgin Birth itself. And from that arises the ultimate question whether such doubts do not go far to invalidate the fundamental Christian doctrine of the Incarnation. Could we still keep Christmas if the Annunciation were to disappear and there were no angels, shepherds or magi? If we are thoroughly to demythologise the gospels will not the whole of the *kerygma*, fact as well as interpretation, disappear?

It is well to ask this question because of the present tendency among some scholars and preachers to start their positive presentation of Christianity, not from the alleged facts of the gospels, but from the *kerygma*. But it is well to remember that the *kerygma* itself contains the outstanding facts of the gospels. Is not the *kerygma* by derivation and definition the proclamation of the saving acts of God? It is not just doctrine with no historical strings attached. It is fact plus interpretation. And that is not a bad description of history itself, as it is commonly written.

We behave therefore quite legitimately if we protest against the method of some apologists who suggest that, in view of the impossibility of deciding whether any words or acts attributed to Jesus are really his, it is best to begin where the early Church itself began, with the *kerygma*. That is a double mistake. First, as we have just seen, you do not get rid that way of the necessity to deal with the historical facts. And second, that is not where the early Church began. If we are to continue to talk of the *kerygma* as a carefully edited manifesto, as we have tended to do ever since C. H. Dodd's introduction of the term to English readers in 1936,[7] the Church could obviously not have begun with it. What the Church began with was a heterogeneous mass of recollections

128

and traditions about Jesus; and what the preachers did was to condense them by constant repetition and selection into the handy collection most suitable for their own purposes. It is we who have formed the current notion of the *kerygma* by combining what we can discover of their collections together and making a systematic outline from the least common multiple.

The real value of the *kerygma* to us is that it shows what the early Church considered to be the heart of its gospel. Every preacher has really only one sermon to preach. The truths that mean all the world to him can be expressed on half a sheet of notepaper, and they recur under various forms in every sermon he preaches : all the rest is embroidery and illustration. It is this essential core of the preaching that Dodd deduced, for instance, from Acts and Paul. A very solutary exercise, but not one that excuses us from the effort to discover the historical base of Christianity and to estimate its proper importance.

Notes

[1] Nevertheless one must continue with the attempt. Even the traditional *cursus vitae* must be nearer the truth than no order at all.

[2] S.P.C.K., 1967.

[3] S.P.C.K., 1969.

[4] The present writer once brought back a rather amusing story from Australia, and produced it in an after-dinner speech in the City. A week or two later, he had the satisfaction of hearing the story reproduced by another speaker at another dinner and confidently attributed to Winston Churchill!

[5] *Kerygma* is distinguished from *didache* as proclamation from instruction.

[6] Luke 2: 2, John 19: 14.

[7] *The Apostolic Preaching and Its Developments* (Hodder and Stoughton). Piecing together Acts and the Pauline epistles Dodd derives the following as the core of the *kerygma:* 1, Prophecies in the scriptures; 2, God sends his servant Jesus; 3, Jesus crucified; 4, Jesus raised from the dead; 5, Jesus exalted bestows his Spirit; 6, The coming Parousia and Judgment; 7, Repent now for the remission of your sins.

10

History in the Evangelists

We must now try to examine, more closely than we have done hitherto, the question of historicity in the gospels. After all, it is they that are generally reckoned as our chief historical source for the life of Jesus. We must ask how far their authors took themselves seriously as historians, and also how justified any such claim could be.

For this purpose we shall commit the apparent solecism of taking the fourth gospel first. The reason for so doing is precisely that it was published last. It may therefore be regarded as the most developed example of the gospel type: whatever tendencies are present in the earlier gospels may be expected to have reached their most obvious fruition in this the latest of the canonical gospels. Obviously we are not likely to find this expectation wholly fulfilled, for no doubt some traits of the earlier gospels will not have justified themselves and so will have disappeared, while others may have been due to the idiosyncrasy of a particular writer and so have been unrepeatable, while again others may have simply failed to appeal to the later author. In spite of all this there should still be enough in the character of the fourth gospel to enable us to discern the development of traits that we remember from the other three.

We begin by reminding ourselves of the declared purpose

for which John was written: "that you may believe that Jesus is the Messiah, the Son of God, and that believing you may have life in his name" (20:31). In other words this is a piece of deliberate propaganda on behalf of the Messiahship of Jesus, because the writer believes that only as one accepts that all-important fact can one be in the way of salvation. The book is very far, then, from being an academic exercise in history or philosophy. The author is more of a preacher in his pulpit than a professor in his lecture-room. The history taught by both preacher and professor may be correct enough, but one would expect the preacher's to be more one-sided than the other's, or at any rate to be suggestive of a more highly particularised point of view.

This description of the writer's purpose does not mean that the book was written solely or even primarily for outsiders. There are indications that it was intended to circulate among churchmen and such as knew already some of the synoptists or at least the traditions represented by them. That is why the author can sometimes refrain from retelling the story of a particular event while at the same time preaching a considerable sermon upon it. Think, for instance, of the institution of the Eucharist which is omitted, and the discourse about it given proleptically in chapter 6; and of the transfiguration, which may be barely alluded to in 1:14 and 12:28–30 but whose spirit pervades the whole book. Most conspicuously of all stands out the story of the baptism, where, in the midst of much explanation, the actual fact of Jesus' own baptism is not mentioned at all (1:29–35).

It has often been debated how well 'John' himself knew the synoptics. Certainly there is no question here of the sort of literary dependence that one gets in the synoptists themselves. The general outline of the story of Jesus is the same although there is much difference in detail (for example the cleansing of the Temple is put early in the ministry instead of late and the timing of the Last Supper is different). The style of writing presents a great contrast to that of the synoptists. The author of the fourth gospel has the most individual style of any New Testament writer, and there are no important passages in his book that could have been lifted bodily from the other gospels. An exception might conceivably be made in the case of the well-known 'Johannine' passage from Q describing Jesus' outburst of praise after the return of the Seventy (Luke 10:21–24, cf. Matt. 11:27 ff.), which seems to have many echoes in John 17. But this is normally regarded by critics as an incursion of Johannine thought into the earlier narrative. How it got there is unexplained; except on the hypothesis that it belonged to some early hymn or else received a liturgical shape in some church whose worship provided a common background for both Q and John.

On the whole it seems likely that the author of the fourth gospel was familiar with the work of his predecessors and set out deliberately to improve upon it. This he may have thought to do, not only by presenting a more carefully meditated and complete doctrine of the incarnation, but also by actually correcting or at least expanding some of the synoptists' historical data. Thus it is he who tells us of the three separate feasts that drew Jesus to Jerusalem (2:13, 5:1, 7:10), so encouraging us to think of a more extended ministry than we might otherwise have envisaged. He appears to be setting the synoptists right when he tells us that Jesus was crucified at the very time when the Passover

133

Lamb was being slain (19:14, 31), whereas from the synoptists we might have concluded that this was the day and the hour of the Last Supper. As an instance of additional detailed information supplied by this writer we may cite the mention of Philip and Andrew as playing specific parts in connection with the feeding of the five thousand (6:7–8).

How far these statements are sufficient to establish the author as an independent and reliable authority is, no doubt, a matter for debate. But there are some hints that would seem to lend verisimilitude to such a view. The tendency of nineteenth-century critics to put the gospel late, well into the second century, has been perforce abandoned. A papyrus fragment (18:31–33; 37–38), discovered in Egypt in 1933 and now in the Rylands Library at Manchester, is generally dated by palaeographists at between A.D. 125 and 130. Three decades would perhaps be enough to allow for the writing, duplication and wide distribution of the original text: we are thus taken back in or near to the first century for its origin. This conclusion may be partially confirmed by traces of an oriental rather than a Greek original text. Although the attempt to prove that it was actually written in Aramaic has proved abortive, scholars are conscious that the author seems to have *thought* in Aramaic and that this may account for the roughness of his Greek. Also we must remember that the person who wrote the appendix (21) was firmly persuaded that the author was none other than the Beloved Disciple himself and therefore, of course, an eyewitness of many of the events he describes (21:24). Even if we find it difficult to accept the redactor's statement as it stands, it must strengthen our faith in the author as an early and authoritative writer.[1]

134

If we turn from the factual narrative to the discourses, the first thing we notice is that the style does not alter to any appreciable degree. The author's idiosyncrasies are maintained alike in stories and speeches; there is no attempt to get into the skin of each actor in the drama and make him speak in the tones proper to his character. Although at first sight this habit may seem to detract from the author's guarantee as a reliable reporter, it should on second thoughts give us a definite regard for his candour. He never puts on an act. He has no need to, because he is quite confident that he is conveying the true sense both of what happened and of what was said.

So in the discourses, some of them quite long, the words are evidently those of the writer but the thoughts he conveys he clearly believes to be the thoughts of Jesus. Even in what appear to be reproductions of the shorter and most characteristic pieces of the synoptics, namely the parables, the story style disappears and is replaced by realistic similes. The good shepherd, the light of the sun, the vine and its branches take the place of the vivid tales that were the delight of the multitudes. But the similes are much more sophisticated and they are much shorter: they are more likely to appeal to the intelligentsia, especially to that part of it that had imbibed some smattering of current Hellenistic philosophy.

Indeed ideas are much more to the front in this than in the other gospels. It has frequently been noticed how often the terms Life, Light, Love occur; and behind them is always the thought of knowledge (*gnosis*)—to know God is the highest of all possibilities. And beyond that again is the all-pervading thought of the incarnation, the eternal Logos, the reason of

God, embodying itself in a word and the Word becoming flesh and settling among men and bringing them the opportunity of retracing their steps to God.

Here is the real difference between the fourth gospel and the synoptics. The author of this book has meditated long and profoundly on the events of the life of his Master, the same events as are given by the synoptists, and he wishes to display their inner meaning. The synoptists, a decade or two earlier, were content for the most part to let the events speak for themselves, with only a little manipulation to bring out the teaching.

By the time of John a new generation is arising, they want to understand why those things were so. They are not so fact-bound as their Jewish parents. They are not content merely to be able to recite the wonderful acts of God. They want to know the rationale of those acts and the character of the God who found expression in them. They want, in other words some reconciliation of the contrasted Hebrew and Greek ways of looking at things, which they had found in the double world of their Hellenistic conceptual environment.

That reconciliation John finds in the key-thought of the eternal Logos made flesh, and he proceeds to reproduce it for them in every line of his book. Paul had made much the same endeavour in his series of letters. Those epistles were mostly answers to specific questions arising out of particular occasions; but Paul had seized the opportunity to carry every question back to first principles. That was, no doubt, the best way to tackle them for a largely Gentile audience. But John's opposite method, the deduction from one primary principle of his meditation upon a series of events, was the better method for his, mostly Jewish, readers.

We can see how he displays this method in his habit of using events as occasions of discourse. The feeding of the five thousand (ch. 6), as we have seen, opens up a discourse on the manna and the bread of life which would inevitably remind his readers of the Last Supper and the Eucharist. A more complex instance is to be found in chapter 9, the healing of the blind man, of which Barrett says, "The foundation of this chapter is twofold: a simple miracle story in which blindness is cured, and the saying, I am the light of the world. The miracle is an efficacious sign of the truth of the saying."[2] Actually it culminates in convicting the Pharisees themselves of blindness and leads on in the next chapter to the great discourse on the door of the sheepfold and the good shepherd.

From this habit of leading from events into discourses it was an easy progression to use the events themselves, particularly miracles, as signs. Indeed in this gospel nothing is just itself, it is also symbolic of something else. Like a modern dramatist, John expects his work to be interpreted at more than one level. The 'temple' is both the stone building in Jerusalem and also the physical integument and instrument of Jesus' personality, his body. Jesus himself is the Lamb of God that is to be slain for the redemption of mankind. The 153 fish represent the varied races of humanity, and the net in which they are caught is the Church on earth.

But the argument must not be pushed too far. It is not likely that the author invented events to make them serve as signs. He is too wedded to historical reality for that. And of all the events used as the bases for signs the greatest and uniquely fundamental one is Jesus himself. As Dodd says, we "recognise the *differentia* of Johannine teaching in the fact that it finds the eternal reality conclusively revealed and embodied in an historical Person, who actually lived, worked, taught, suffered and died, with actual and direct historical consequences. . . . It follows that it is important for the evangelist that what he narrates happened."[3]

The well-known description of the fourth as the *spiritual* gospel is obviously not far short of the mark. It is certainly part of the author's purpose to show how the absolute is linked with time. That is why there is no apocalyptic eschatology in this book. Eternity is not conceived as bursting in upon us in a great cataclysm at the end of time; it pervades the whole of time and makes itself felt in every temporal incident. As George Moore once said, "The future does not come from before to meet us, but streams up from behind over our heads." The fourth evangelist's idea of eternity is something even more pervasive—a universal reality in which time is immersed like a sponge in the sea. Perhaps the best epithet to apply to his attitude would be 'sacramental'. He was, as we have seen, particularly interested in baptism and the Eucharist: they gave him the clue for the understanding of the constitution of all things. As baptism conveyed the Spirit and the Eucharist the personality of Christ, so the physical universe as a whole is an effective sign of spiritual reality. This constitution of matter achieved its apotheosis when the Word was made Flesh; from that peak its influence flowed down through all subsequent events bringing living waters of grace and truth.

No one would deny that this way of looking at things has some small measure of affinity with the type of thought that was later known as Gnosticism. The tendency to let the theology take charge of the history; the interest in *gnosis* or knowledge; the emphasis on redemption; the personification of ideas like Truth, Life, Light, Love are all typical of this kind of thought. But when this gospel was written Gnosticism was at a very inchoate stage; it was not yet formulated; it had not yet become the avowed enemy of the Church. Paul and John himself were aware of the danger and tried in their letters to wean their readers away from its temptation. Its dissolution of history, its cultivation of superiority, its fondness for angelic and demonic genealogies, its paradoxical proneness to sins of the flesh: these all mark the distinction between gnosticism and the gospel. It had a strong appeal to all who had a leaning towards esoteric doctrines and practices or were prepared to ape learning by turning their religion into pseudo-philosophy. By the middle of the second century A.D. it had become a series of carefully articulated, if fantastic, systems; but in the first it was only with difficulty that it could be given a name at all. Nevertheless some scholars have gone so far as to describe the fourth gospel as a gnostic drama. If accepted, the effect of such a characterisation would be to undermine all faith in the historical Christianity of this gospel, for the Gnostics had no particular interest in the 'facts' of history and were quite ready to regard them as merely symbolic. They even tended to take a docetic view of the person of Jesus himself and would not allow that the Christ had ever suffered upon a cross. The most casual reader must see at once how different is all this from the spirit of the fourth gospel.

We conclude then that the gospel of John is in general a reliable historical source, but that it is more interested in drawing out the meaning of history than in recording chronological facts; that it expects to be read with an eye to the eternal truth embodied in the temporal event; that its effect is to show how the Absolute is revealed in time; and that its intent is to proclaim the saving truth of the love, life and glory of God revealed in the humiliation of Jesus.

Having thus looked at the fourth gospel we can now go back and examine the first, not the first in canonical order but the one that is generally accepted as the first in time, St. Mark. This work is especially important because it actually inaugurated the new type of literature, the gospel, the proclamation of good news.[4] The later gospels follow this model, although they try to improve upon it. But St. Mark's, just because it was the first, should help us to understand both what a gospel was meant to be and how the author viewed the material of which he had to make use. Our actual dating of Mark will depend largely upon our view of chapter 13, whether we think it shows signs of having been written after the siege of Jerusalem rather than before. If it does, then we shall date the book soon after A.D. 70: if it does not, then we shall put it somewhere between A.D. 60 and 70. In any case it preceded the fourth gospel by two or three decades.

To judge from the shape of the Marcan book we should say that a gospel was intended to be a narrative of the sufferings, death and resurrection of Jesus together with some preliminary account of his ministry. This model is still observable in all the other three gospels: they differ in detail but all preserve this main outline and all set forth the challenge conveyed in the 'good news' of the redemption won by Christ.

All agree in devoting a large proportion of their space to the account of the passion. It has even been suggested that a separate narrative of the end of the Lord's earthly life circulated quite early among the churches and was used as a quarry by our evangelists. Whether this is true or not, it seems certain that Mark's was the first written continuous story of the whole ministry. It is now generally agreed that what Mark had to go upon (apart from the passion narrative) when he wrote his gospel was a series of unconnected short stories about Jesus stored up in the tradition of the Church and repeated orally so often that their language had become stereotyped and polished. Mark chose whichever of these fragments best suited his purpose and connected them together as best he could, but not necessarily in chronological order. Obviously what we have here is no biography—a gospel is not, and is not intended to be, a biography. Whether it furnishes material for a biography is another story.

Attention will inevitably be focussed upon the fragments, the unconnected short pieces or 'forms' as they are called. It is they that point back beyond the written records in which they have been incorporated and give us the nearest approach we have to first-hand knowledge of Jesus. They do not, however, in themselves give us much information about the writer, except in so far as we may learn something from his choice of items. To learn about him and his views we must look closely at the framework in which he sets each of the so-called forms. Modern ingenuity has gone a long way towards isolating the framework within which each evangelist has set the fragments composing the mosaic of his total work. Subsequent investigation has given us an opportunity of comparing the views of the evangelist as displayed in the framework with those of the texts he has incorporated. But it can safely be said that so far there has been found no vital difference between them. The evangelist often gives a twist to the interpretation of a story or a parable to meet the condition of his own times, as any preacher does. But the Jesus of the evangelist is still demonstrably the same as the Jesus of the earlier tradition.[5]

Here there is a certain difference between the earliest and the latest of the gospels. In Mark the fact and its interpretation are set side by side, or at least the fact is put within its interpretative frame. But in 'John' the interpretation has, so to speak, absorbed the fact. The process has been made all the easier because the writer, as already pointed out, has only one style in composition, and assimilates the language of all his characters to his own. Mark is nearer the origin of the Christian message in keeping them distinct. But John shows himself nearer the heart of it through seeing so clearly the inner meaning of what happens and not being too cautious to make it known. In John there are few 'forms' but much interpretation: in Mark there are many forms but little interpretation. The one is introvert and the other extrovert. But the truth they see is the same.

An instance (taken entirely at random) of the difference in method can be seen in the respective ways in which the two authors approach the Feeding of the Five Thousand (Mark 6:30, John 6:1–5). Mark begins his section at the return of the apostles from their mission. They come from their various tasks and report to Jesus, who says that they must be tired and that they need to get away from the crowds. So they embark in the boat and make for a deserted spot. The people, however, detect the move. When Jesus disembarked he

142

found a crowd awaiting him, and was moved to pity because they seemed so lost. He continued teaching them for the rest of the day until, in the late evening, his disciples suggested that it would be wise to dismiss them so that before dark they could go to the neighbouring villages and buy food. But he replies to the disciples that they must themselves provide the necessary food.

This account reads like a piece of good, straightforward journalistic reporting. It reveals the writer's own interests only in the way the story is narrated. The disciples' confidence in their Master is shown by the naturalness with which they tell him the result of their efforts, while his concern is for their tiredness and hunger. Jesus would like to escape the crowds, but fails in his attempt, largely because he is so sorry for them. His compassion is further shown in his anxiety to feed them on the spot. As far as this extract is concerned, Mark gives what the journalists call a thoroughly 'human' story. The only suggestion of something out of the common is the calmness with which Jesus faces the responsibility for feeding so large a body of people.

John's narrative is very different. He does not mention the apostles' mission as a starting-point, but simply begins 'After these things'. All he tells us is that Jesus went to the other side of the sea (identifying it as the sea of Galilee or Tiberias). A great crowd followed him because they had seen some of his healing miracles. This accords with John's interest in the analysis of belief. Here he shows how people can first be attracted to Christ by his ministrations to the sick. It is only a beginning but it may ripen later into true faith.

Then, we are told, Jesus went up into 'the mountain'. What mountain is not specified, nor does it matter. John is

143

setting the scene for what is to follow. Jesus is on rising ground where he can be most easily heard and seen. His disciples are grouped immediately around him. Here the author inserts a note of time: "Now the passover, the feast of the Jews, was at hand." But it is not intended as a hint of chronology: it is meant to strike a theological note and to prepare the way for the coming 'sign', and its association with the manna, the bread of life, the Last Supper and the Eucharist, all of which are to be explained in the coming discourse.

It is then that Jesus lifts up his eyes and sees a vast multitude approaching. Immediately he asks Philip what they are going to do about feeding so great a company. He does not wait for his disciples to take the initiative. He is the Word made flesh, the eternal Logos in human nature: it is right that the initiative should come from him. It is not that he had any need to ask for information. He puts the question to Philip merely to test him and to give him a lesson in the necessity of trust—another example of John's preoccupation with the question of developing faith.

We have thus in a random example a fairly good illustration of the way in which two evangelists handled the same piece of tradition and how they treated history. Whether Mark really drew his information direct from Peter or not, his account certainly reads much more like that of an eyewitness than the other. John too is vivid enough, but his vividness is more that of one who has pondered so much and so long over the event that it has re-created itself in his mind's eye and all the details have become expressive of his own particular attitude of mind. Both writers grasp the essential facts, but John at least seems to exercise a certain freedom with the details. Mark's narrative is like a sharp-toothed crag recently erupted from the sea while John's is the same crag after it has been smoothed over by wind and ice and tide. But the crag is the same; and it is manifestly the same Jesus who is seen at work in both narratives.

Turning now to the third gospel we can see how Luke handled the same piece of tradition. He sticks more closely to Mark's order than John in that he begins from the return of the apostolic missioners, but he reduces Mark's account considerably. The apostles return and report, that is all. Then Jesus 'took them and withdrew apart'. There is the bare fact, but Mark's reference to the busy traffic at their home base is deliberately omitted and there is no reference to the lake or to the boat. On the other hand there is no suggestion that Jesus tried to avoid the crowds. Rather it was to a 'city', Bethsaida, that he withdrew and when the multitudes followed him he actually welcomed them and spent the day teaching them about the Kingdom of God and healing those who needed his attention (this last an addition to Mark).

Similarly, Luke agrees with Mark that it was from the disciples that the suggestion first came to send the people away to get food, but Jesus replied, "Give ye them to eat." These adaptations do not seem of epoch-making significance, but they do fit in very well with Luke's consistent picture of Jesus as the calm, dignified benefactor of society, a little less intimate and personal than in the other gospels. But then Luke is writing for a dignified Roman or Romanised official, and he comes as near as possible to making his hero wear a toga. So Jesus is not here the Galilean peasant. He is the leader, very much in command of the situation. Yet he is recognisably the same Jesus that we have in Mark and in

John. The portrait is sketched from a different angle, that is all.

If we had had time and space it would have been interesting to go further into the question of Luke's view of history as revealed in his editing of the forms he took over either from Mark or from Q or else from some source of his own. The work carried out recently in the field of this 'redaction criticism', has done something to modify the opinion formerly held that Luke is a purely objective historian. That was the impression derived from his own statement in his preface about his careful resort to a comparative study of the relevant documents before beginning to write his gospel. This seemed so like the modern method of working that critics were ready to conclude that Luke was the nearest approach to a professional historian that we have in the New Testament.

Recent examination of the framework in which he placed the many vignettes gathered from other sources reveals St. Luke as at least as much theologian as historian: he is quite prepared to interpret or introduce the facts in such a way as to bring out what he conceives to be their real spiritual import. Thus Luke in the transfiguration story emphasises more than the other synoptists the 'glory' of Jesus (9:31, 32) combined with the premonition of the 'exodus' which he is to accomplish at Jerusalem (9:31), and he leaves more open than the others the possibility that the whole occurrence was more in the nature of a vision than a physical reality.

Similarly if we examine the three versions of the temptation story[6] (which is not mentioned in the fourth gospel at all), we shall see tendencies at work which ultimately made the writing of the 'spiritual gospel' possible. Mark's brief, horrendous, almost barbaric account of this great decisive conflict between Jesus and Satan follows immediately upon the record of Jesus' baptism. Luke inserts between the two events a long genealogical tree. It is not easy to see why — unless it is to establish that he who is to be tempted was a legal descendant of the great King David and indeed came primarily down from God.

In their accounts Matthew and Luke appear to rely upon Q rather than Mark, and both give details of three separate temptations. Luke says that Jesus came from the Jordan 'full of the Holy Spirit', by whom he was afterwards led up and down the wilderness forty days being constantly tempted by the Devil. At the end of the three named temptations the Devil, according to Luke, departs, but only for a season. He bides his time and will surely come again. We notice again Luke's independence, his polite polish over against the grim vividness of Mark, his concern for the dignity of Jesus and his emphasis on the close association between Jesus and the Holy Spirit. Matthew's general attitude agrees with Luke's, and the fact that he has a different order for the two last temptations hardly appears significant.

Like Luke, Matthew elsewhere adds a theological interest to the bare narration of Mark. Thus in the case of the parable of the sower,[7] which is a picture of an everyday event, Matthew sees the sower as Jesus, and the seed as his 'word of the kingdom'.[8] But he also sees the seed as the various types of hearer, that is the average member of the Church (v. 19). The lesson of the parable therefore becomes one of encouragement to Matthew's own contemporaries, the struggling congregation: they will have considerable success

147

in their fundamental work of mission if they persevere, in spite of heavy and repeated losses.

More significant is the care with which, in the explanation of the parable (v. 13), Matthew tones down the seemingly harsh statement found in both Mark (4:12) and Luke (8:10) that Jesus spoke in parables in order to prevent people from understanding him. On the contrary, Matthew's version implies, parables are necessary because people are too dull to understand without them. To prevent the possibility of further misunderstanding he quotes, in a gentler form, the passage (Isaiah 6:9, 10) from which the original assertion appears to have been taken. Such specimens may fairly be taken as typical of much else in the gospels.

From this discussion, however slight and inadequate, certain conclusions as to the aims of the evangelists and the nature of their work begin to emerge. In the first place we recognise that the gulf between the fourth gospel and the other three is not nearly so wide as used to be thought: the fourth merely carries further certain tendencies already discernible in the others. At the same time the fact that the tendencies are so obvious in the fourth helps us to identify them even in their embryonic state in the earlier three.

Perhaps the most important trait that comes out in each one is its independence. This can be said in spite of an equally obvious trait, namely their dependence (apart from Mark) on each other. It may not be possible to say precisely who had read whom, though it is as certain as anything can be that Matthew and Luke had read Mark. Even Mark, who, if his really was the model and the earliest gospel, had not had the opportunity to read the others, nevertheless had access to many well-established traditions, which the others may also have later known in a variety of versions. Some scholars, who are not prepared to agree that John knew any of the other gospels, are yet prepared to accept the suggestion that he was aware of the traditions from which they had drawn their information.

This dependence upon predecessors does not destroy their essential independence. Each one probably had sources to draw upon which were unknown to the others. Certainly Matthew and Luke had each his own tradition of the birth narratives. And John may have been relying on his own sources of information when he appears to be deliberately correcting the synoptists. Thus what is perhaps of equal importance from our present angle is that each of the evangelists had his own independent point of view.

One of the most engrossing employments of biblical theologians in recent decades has been the task of showing how each evangelist differs from the rest in the detailed picture of Jesus, of his work and teaching, of his attitude to the people and of their reaction to him. So far has the somewhat disintegrating process of this analysis gone in recent years that we are warned not only against trying to write a biography of Jesus but even against trying to paint a portrait of him. This, however, is to carry caution too far. Each evangelist has his own portrait of Jesus, but they are obviously portraits of the same man, and we feel that we know him all the better from being able to view him from several different angles.

Individual independence is shown in choice of themes and incidents, in the general purpose of writing, in the arrange-

ment of material and in the addition, omission and adaptation
of details to serve the purpose of the overall aim of the
writer. We can notice a mounting confidence on the part of
the authors as we proceed from the earliest to the latest.
In Mark there is little set interpretation: he lets the story
tell itself. The proportion of interpretation to fact increases
with successive gospels until in the fourth we get comparatively few isolated incidents but a great wealth of
interpretation.

Similarly with regard to the contrast in governing themes,
to which we have already drawn attention. In Mark such a
special theme is not easy to find: a modern suggestion is that
the work is intended to describe the life of Jesus as the focal
point of the struggle between God and the demon world. Or
the purpose may have been just to record what was known
of Jesus' life and ministry before it lost its clear outline in the
land of myth and legend. The aim of Matthew was to depict
the Messiah and his continuing Church. The aim of Luke, as
stated by himself, was to produce an authenticated story for
an intelligent and cultured Roman. The aim of the fourth
gospel was to win readers to life-giving faith in Jesus as Son
of God. In pursuance of these aims all the writers show
individual theological and Christological leanings. It would
be more possible to show a staged progression in this kind of
propensity, if it were easier to decide on the respective dates
of Matthew and Luke. But at least it can be asserted without
fear of contradiction that there is such a progression and that,
as far as the New Testament is concerned, it reveals its
opposite extremes in Mark and John.

Frank recognition of this situation helps us in our evalua-
tion of the evangelists as historians. We cannot divide them

any longer into three historians and one theologian. All of them have a real regard for facts. All of them are capable of using facts as symbols. All of them may be suspected on occasion of using symbols as if they were facts. All of them have an eye on the religious implications of what they write. All of them are much more interested in religion than in the chronicle of events. All of them have their particular and individual reason for writing. All of them share a desire to show the life and teaching of Jesus as relevant to their own contemporaries. In other words they are all preachers and theologians as well as historians.

We recognise then that the kind of history we get in the gospels is not the sort we get, or look for, in modern textbooks, which struggle after objectivity and ignore the supernatural. But from the religious point of view it may be none the worse for that. Indeed it may perhaps be best described as religious history, in spite of the objections that may be raised to the term and of the scorn it may arouse in the mind of any who would take it as implying that it is no history at all. It is in fact good history of its own kind. It is characteristic of its own period. It gives us the facts as it sees them and puts its own interpretation upon them. But it is perfectly honest in letting us see how it arrives at its interpretation. It is quite candid about the change of understanding that took place after Jesus' resurrection. It does not conceal the early quarrels of the apostles, nor the human weariness of Jesus, nor the doubts that even those nearest to him felt about his person and work.

We could enlarge our view of this general tendency if we showed how individual evangelists sometimes suppress or modify what they have read in others. Thus in the story of

Peter's confession Matthew amplifies Mark's account (8:27–30) by explaining the term 'Christ' as meaning 'Son of the Living God', and adds the promise to Peter, who has made the confession, that he shall be the rock upon which the Church shall be built (Matt. 16:13–20). Again Matthew modifies Mark's absolute prohibition of marriage after divorce (Mark 10:11–12) by allowing a specific exception in the case of 'fornication' (Matt. 19:9, cf. 5:32).

Similarly Luke has his own interests to serve in correcting or improving Mark. Thus he gives an explanation of the inauguration of Jesus' mission (Luke 4:21) as a fulfilment of prophecy. Writing for a Roman he enumerates the three charges brought against Jesus in Pilate's court (23:2), which Mark had left vague. Again he shows his special interest in the Samaritans by adding to Mark's gospel the parable of the Good Samaritan and the narrative of the ten lepers, of whom the only grateful one was a Samaritan (10:30–37; 17:11–19).

An instance of difference in the treatment of a source document (Q?) which Matthew and Luke share in common can be seen in the latter's blessing on the poor (6:20) who in Matthew become piously 'the poor in spirit' (5:3), and upon the hungry (Luke 6:21) who in Matthew 5:6 are described with similar piety as those who 'hunger and thirst after righteousness'. It would perhaps be too crude to describe the respective interests of Matthew and Luke as churchly and courtly, but the few instances adduced show how the tendencies suggested by these epithets may have affected the style of the writers concerned. Much the same might be said of their respective choice in the birth narratives and the tables of descent, Matthew being content to take the genealogy back to Abraham the forefather of the covenant people, while Luke takes it right back to Adam, the progenitor of the whole human race, and so to God.

Perhaps the best place in which to study Luke's style is in the great non-Marcan passage 9:51–18:14, where he is either relying on sources outside the other gospels or exercising greater originality. Here we notice particularly the parables of the Good Samaritan, of the Rich Fool, the unfruitful Fig Tree, the Lost Sheep, the Lost Coin, the Lost Son, the Unrighteous Steward, the Rich Man and Lazarus, the Unrighteous Judge, and the Pharisee and Publican. These show an unexpected sense of humour, a homely sympathy with the poor and outcast, and a psychological understanding of the human heart. To these parables, we may add two miracles of healing—of a woman on the Sabbath and of ten lepers including one grateful Samaritan. Among the items of teaching are the exhortation to repentance based on the fate of the slain Galileans (13:1–5), the half-mocking advice to guests and hosts (14:7–14), and the warning of the cost of discipleship (17:7–10). These certainly help to fill out our portrait of the Christ, and they also help to identify him with the person of Jesus of Nazareth.

Here again we find ourselves in a region of mingled narrative and interpretation. The same may be said of those passages which Luke shares with Matthew. Both evangelists may have obtained them from Q (the surmised teaching source), which is believed to have been roughly contemporary with Mark. But so far as style and spirit go, there is nothing to distinguish them from the rest. Nor is there any chance of disentangling here the Jesus of the gospels from a supposedly different and original Jesus who was not surrounded by the magical prestige of a wonderworker and a popular hero. This at least is how the wonderworker appeared to those who wrote about him after his resurrection, and none of us seems to be able to get any further than that, beyond making a few allowances for pardonable exaggeration or misunderstanding.

Of all four gospels we must say that for good or evil they all belong to the same type, with the same combination of factual narrative and theological interpretation, though the proportions of the ingredients differ in each. There are differences also in factual detail, but not such as to affect the general, overall picture. On that truth, in spite or because of, the meticulous examination to which modern science has subjected them, they still stand four-square to make their proclamation to the world. Unless we are prepared to rule out the supernatural in advance, we must acknowledge that they present a serious challenge to our faith.

Notes

[1] R. T. Fortna (*The Gospel of Signs*, C.U.P., 1970) thinks he has isolated the original text as an almost entirely miracle and passion source, written probably in Syria and possibly before A.D. 70 in an attempt to prove that Jesus was the Messiah. The long discourses of our present gospel would have been added later.

[2] C. K. Barrett, *The Gospel according to St. John* (S.P.C.K., 1955), p. 292.

[3] C. H. Dodd, *Interpretation of the Fourth Gospel* (C.U.P., 1953), p. 444.

[4] Discussing the literary nature of a 'gospel', Norman Perrin describes it as current Christian experience of Christ cast in the form of a chronicle of Jesus' ministry. (*What is Redaction Criticism?* S.P.C.K., 1970, p. 75.)

[5] The point has been made that in any case there must have been sufficient congruity between the disciples' recollections of the Man of Nazareth and their experience of the risen Christ to make the post-resurrection Christology feasible.

[6] See Wand, *The Temptation of Jesus* (Sumner Press, 1965).

[7] Matt. 13: 1–23 (cf. Mark 4: 1–20, Luke 8: 4–15).

[8] Cf. above p. 44.

11

Conclusion

Some pages back we were considering whether we could find any way of escape from the dilemma occasioned by two difficulties that confront modern man, (*a*) the prevailing scepticism with regard to historical certainty and (*b*) the acknowledged improbability of proving events in eternity by arguments drawn from time and space.

We paused for a time to consider what amount of verisimilitude was actually provided by the most recent study of the New Testament documents. The answer is likely to be framed in accordance with each student's own predilections. Those who want to feel absolutely firm ground beneath their feet will be likely to say that they do not find it here, while those who are ready to be satisfied with probability as their guide may feel that they have at least sufficient of it to justify an act of faith.

It is possible that this is really as far as we can go. Actually it should be far enough. We have no right to expect that the matters we are dealing with should be provable without any shadow of doubt. We have always been taught that faith is the Christian's *métier*, and here we see the truth of it. If there is no possibility of doubt, what room if left for faith?[1] Faith is a willingness to trust even where there is no logical certainty. The schoolboy's definition, 'Faith means believing what you can't prove', has a certain point. On the other hand, 'Faith is believing what you know is not true', is a cynic's aphorism and quite contradictory to the Christian's standard. If you can prove that a thing is not true, then you obviously cannot believe it, whatever happens.

It would, however, be extremely undesirable to leave the question in this state of nicely balanced doubt, as if there were no preponderance of guide-lines to a satisfactory belief. Perhaps we have not looked closely enough. If scholarship fails to give us a clear judgment, would it not be as well to go back to the Bible and ask whether it has any opinion or example to offer of itself? Is it faced at all with our kind of problem, and if so how does it deal with it?

In so far as our dilemma is a modern one we can hardly expect it to be adumbrated in the Bible, or at least in the Old Testament. The idea of eternity or infinity was not indigenous to Hebrew thought. 'Everlasting' was in any case to the Hebrews an unlimited extension of time rather than an enhanced condition of existence. There can be no doubt, however, about their interest in history. Their whole religion was built upon what they conceived to be concrete facts of the past. The call of Abraham, the crossing of the Red Sea, the covenant at Sinai: these were foundation facts which dictated the whole structure of their religion.

Of the traditional division of the Jewish canon into law, prophets and writings, the middle section includes the books we know as historical, and the legal group also involves much history. But when we speak of 'history' in this connection we must remember with particular care what we have said so often about the close connection in the Bible between fact and interpretation.

Merely to state a plain fact would hardly have seemed to a biblical writer to be worth while. His purpose in writing was not to establish a fact so much as to bring out its meaning. We must not therefore think that the fact is not there: it is there, although it may be overlaid, or perhaps even deformed, by the burden of interpretation laid upon it. All the resources of modern ingenuity and scholarship may be required to get at the precise fact, or at what would be recognised as such by the modern scholar. When it has been found, the inquirer will discover that the writer, or the tradition he is following, has deliberately used a seemingly secular event to illustrate the dealings of God with his chosen people for their benefit and for that of the whole world.

We are at the moment confronted by two quite different versions of Israel's history. First there is that which the biblical writers themselves give of a race founded, ruled and guided by God for their own salvation and the good of mankind, and there is a second which the scientific historian is endeavouring to draw out without any reference to God or the supernatural. In the former case a definite pattern is discovered in the course of events, which are shown to reveal the overruling providence of God. In the second, an overall pattern becomes increasingly difficult to find as learning increases the number of secular possibilities and as even the once fashionable theory of universal evolution seems to be dropping out of favour, at least in so far as it affects Jewish religion. In any case it is to be noted that the biblical writers are as careful to establish facts as are modern historians, though their methods may be less precise.

Thus it is upon certain decisive events that the story of salvation is built. The call of Abraham is not just an episode

Conclusion

in tribal migration, but the divine choice of one family to become a vehicle of blessing for all nations. The crossing of the Red Sea is not so much a striking natural phenomenon as a means of delivering the chosen family, now become a considerable clan, from a grave danger to its existence, and also as an introduction to its future nationhood. The eruption on Mount Sinai is seen to give an appropriate natural setting for the solemn covenant between Jehovah and his people, which will settle their mutual relations for ever and decide the law by which God's people shall live.

This propensity for seeing the hand of God in the historic events of the ages, turning everything to the salvation of his people and the consequent benefit of mankind, was carefully cultivated by writers down the ages. You can see it in some of the prophets, but more particularly in the psalmists, who often run over the outstanding events in past history, showing how God has turned them to his purposes. At least twenty Psalms have this as their theme, but one can see it especially in Psalms 66, 78, 81, 135, 136.

The habit of choosing out the high spots of Israelite history and interpreting them as evidence of divine providence was continued into the New Testament period. The most conspicuous evidence of the habit is to be found in the speeches of Stephen, Peter and Paul in Acts. These speeches differ from the Old Testament because to the list of the 'mighty acts' of God they add the passion and resurrection of Jesus Christ. Such additions involve a drastic remodelling of the story of salvation. They stand themselves at the heart of the new Christian 'gospel': the Old Testament story is now interpreted as a premonition of the story of Christ, and the Christ story is seen as a fulfilment of prophecy. The whole account of salvation has thus become an unit, historically based but now a challenge from the spiritual sphere to all men of good will, offering a glorious future in time and in eternity.

There can be no doubt that the bulk of the first Christian preaching was based on this scheme. It is to such a presentation of the Christian case that the name *kerygma* or 'proclamation' is given in modern reconstructions. As Koch says, "*Kerygma* means the announcement of divine action exhorting the hearer to faith."[2] This style became the manner in which Christians communicated with each other and with the outside world. It was certainly the way in which they thought of the past both immediate and long-term. No doubt, in the more intimate preaching or catechising among themselves many details would be fitted into this general outline. Many traditions relating to the life and death of Jesus, his wonderful birth, his baptism and transfiguration, his miracles and teaching, his call of the disciples and appointment of the apostles, his crucifixion and rising from the dead would all be elaborated, and would ultimately form the basis of the gospels. But always the historical facts would be interpreted with an eye to edification.

It is important to recognise that this is the only kind of history we have in the New Testament or indeed anywhere in the Bible.[3] Some would say that it is the most worthwhile history there is, but it is not the kind of history that commends itself to the professional historian. The latter, if he wishes to get at the 'bare' facts, must dig very deep, and there are some philosophers who say that success is impossible. That is at least one reason why the 'search for the historical Jesus' has been so widely abandoned.

Conclusion

The task has certainly not been made easier by the first-century writers' habit of incorporating para-historical material, myth and legend into their story. In accordance with the habit of their time that does not seem to have mattered to them so long as they could use it as a basis for the exhortation. If these accumulating traditions possessed a certain air of verisimilitude, they probably went in with the rest without too many questions being asked except that of edification. In spite of the claims of St. Luke we must stop thinking of the writers of the New Testament as if they were university professors.

This method of dealing with events does not mean, as some would suppose, that the *kerygma* is sheer myth in the sense of fiction. On the contrary, it emphasises the factual importance of the main constituents of the preaching. In the New Testament a firm grasp of the actual flesh-and-blood existence of Jesus, his birth, crucifixion and resurrection, dominates everything else.[4] These are the facts of history about which there is no vagueness or hesitation. It is because they are so well established and so important that a certain amount of legendary matter inevitably gathers around them: small wonder if we cannot always distinguish clearly between what is strictly factual in this additional material and what is hagiology, edification or propaganda.

What is more important is that these writers have not been able to carry forward the salvation-history of their people without recognising in Jesus of Nazareth the promised Messiah and Son of God. Here in Jesus the long history that began with the call of Abraham has come to the turning-point, it cannot be that he in whom world history is so centred can be himself less than divine. In connection with him a new series of mighty acts has been begun to make clear the way in which God saves his people.

Jesus' own resurrection and ascension, the descent of the Holy Spirit at Pentecost, to say nothing of many detailed deliverances of leading personalities among the early leaders, these all demonstrated that God was still working through concrete acts for the delivery of his people. It was true that the number affected was miserably small. Indeed at one moment when 'they all forsook him and fled', it could have been said that Jesus himself was the sole representative of the Kingdom. Nevertheless the believers in the Christ affirmed that they and they only were the true inheritors of the promises made to the fathers. When the nation as a whole refused to accept the claims of Jesus, it forfeited the right to call itself the people of God. The followers of the Christ became exclusively the true 'Israel', and it was along their line that the history of salvation continued its course.

These considerations should show that the Bible is at least consistent in its view of history. It claims all history and particularly that of Israel as the field for the working out of the purposes of God. The outstanding events of history show with special clarity the hand of God shaping the destinies of the nations for the salvation of his chosen people and the ultimate benefit of the whole world.

Paul will presently have to meet the argument that his ancient people, the Jews, seem on this showing to have lost their privileged position, and that thereby God is revealed as having failed to keep his promise. But Paul will try to show that this is not God's fault: the Jews themselves rejected the promises as they were being fulfilled in Christ. In any case the defection of the Jews is only for a period, permitted by

Conclusion

Providence to give the Gentiles a chance to hear the gospel. Then, when they have received it, the Jews will be moved to emulation and will learn to claim their own inheritance.

This may seem glib and naïve, but Paul was wrestling with an apparently intractable problem. It was not easy to offer the world a religion of salvation, which had come from the Jews, but which the Jews themselves had manifestly rejected. He was dealing with an existing situation and finding for it the most religious explanation he could. And who shall say that he was wrong? God's honour was vindicated, his promise would be fulfilled, its blessings would be extended to the whole world, and ultimately all his chosen would be saved.

In any case, whether right or wrong, Paul gives us a clear example of the way in which the Bible deals with history. Its method is in marked contrast with our own. When we are writing history we carefully eschew any reference to the supernatural. Even if we are writing church history we stick closely to the institutional side of events: our narration is ecclesiastical rather than spiritual. The Biblical writers had very little interest in that side of things: they were not interested in secondary causes but always went direct to the prime cause, which was God. As someone once said, if they had been describing a bicycle skidding they would not have talked about the effect of H_2O on paving blocks, but would have said quite simply, 'And the Lord took my wheel from under me.' So in history it is always the divine hand that they see.

It is sometimes claimed that this is a quite justifiable way of writing history. If people can write military history or economic history by isolating the military or economic aspect

163

of events, why cannot they write religious history by concentrating on the aspect of salvation? But this is not quite the same thing. Warfare and economics are matters of time and space; in other words they are made of material germane to the same stuff as that of which history in general is made. But the Bible brings into consideration as one of the main constituents of its history something of a quite extraneous nature, something that belongs not to time and space but to the eternal and the absolute.

If it is always the divine hand that the ancients see, what are we to say to those of our contemporaries who cannot see the divine hand at all? There is very little that we can say, except that the biblical view seems to us to offer the better explanation of the universe and of the course it has run. At least there does not seem any other explanation so credible as that which is assumed by the biblical writers. Chance and evolution have undoubtedly played their part; but to suppose that there has been no over-all guidance of events would require belief in miracles greater than any supplied by the Christian story. The strongest evolutionist is hardly likely to be so strict a determinist that he would deny any room for individual free will. And if there is room in the scheme of things for the individual to frame his own purposes, it is hardly likely that there would be no place for a general directive purpose in the universe as a whole. And who could be the originator of such a purpose but God?

In other words we are in much the same position with regard to the divine direction of history as we were with regard to the identification of the Jesus of history with the Christ of faith. We cannot by sheer demonstration bridge the gap between the physical event and the spiritual reality: we have to leap it. Teilhard de Chardin could draw a fascinating picture of the development of *homo sapiens* and of his new start in the *logos incarnatus*, but he could not by his science prove the link between the divine and the human spirit. The link is only obvious to those who are predisposed to see it.

In this respect we are no worse off than those who search for beauty. The fact of beauty can never be proved to us unless we are open to it. Who can prove the beauty in the lingering colours of an autumn woodland, or in the sombre majesty of a Rembrandt portrait, or in the poetry of 'A rose-red city, half as old as time'? The fact that we cannot *prove* any eternal realities behind the superficial show of things does not mean that they are not there. But if the hypothesis that they are there provides the most reasonable explanation of the existing state of things, we have surely every right to pursue our inquiries with an open mind. We shall be prepared to give a sympathetic hearing to the Old Testament writers when they profess to see the hand of God at work in the history of their people, and to the New Testament writers when they see the glory of God reflected in the face of Jesus Christ.

We shall be ready to see how the same God guides the fortunes of his people in both Testaments and especially how he expresses himself in the person of Jesus of Nazareth. Here, if anywhere, there must be a culminating point in the history of salvation. We shall be anxious to see how close is the identity of Jesus the Nazarene with the Christ of traditional orthodoxy.

It must be admitted that one's path at this point is made hazardous by the masochistic desire of some Christian scholars to make their task as difficult as possible for themselves. While still maintaining the identity, they make the historical Jesus appear as unlike the traditional portrait of Christ as possible. Perhaps the words of the prophet "He had no beauty that we should desire him" (Isa. 53:2) have been taken too literally as a prophecy of Christ; or there has been too violent a reaction against the doctrine of the sinlessness of Jesus. In any case it is suggested that so far from seeing in Jesus an admirable figure we should not, if we had been his contemporaries, have liked him at all. That may be perfectly true, but it leaves out of sight the fact that the fault would have been entirely ours. Nor is there the slightest scrap of evidence to suggest, as some recent writers have done, that Jesus may have been a homosexual. The point, however, is worth noticing as an example of the extent to which the modern apologist will lean over backwards in the endeavour not to appear to claim too much for his side. Such scrupulosity is quite unwarranted and can do no more than create unnecessary doubt and confusion. For the vast majority of readers the figure that stands out from the gospels is one of sublime beauty and fascination. If it dismays us, it is because it sets a standard which is so much higher than our own. It witnesses to a life spent entirely for others in dependence upon God. It is the noblest ideal ever set before the human race. It is the picture of human perfection.

That human perfection must still be poles asunder from divinity was axiomatic to the Jew. Nevertheless, looking back after the resurrection, the disciples of Jesus recognised divinity mirrored in the character of their Master, and authors from Paul onwards wrote steadfastly from that point of view. They saw the gulf between the divine and human bridged in Jesus Christ, and they used every argument from their Old Testament books to prove it, reinforcing them with such elements of Greek philosophical wisdom as they had consciously or unconsciously imbibed.

Obviously such arguments can hardly convince us today, although we can see the point of showing how the same God who guided the fortunes of his ancient people was still at work in Christ and in the events that flowed from him. Essentially we are in the same position as those writers were: we have to decide whether we can discern the action of divinity in the history of the Jewish people and in the person of Christ. Certainly we cannot prove it, but we may see that it is not unreasonable. Indeed we may think it far better as a hypothesis than any other theory that the learned world has to offer. That is the nub of the question whether Christianity is a historical religion: was Jesus divine or not, was the Carpenter of Nazareth essentially identical with the Christ of the earliest Christian orthodoxy? If he was, then we can regard Christianity as historical inasmuch as its essential faith has been the same from the beginning of the Church to the present day.[5] About this part of the answer we do not think there is much difference among theological scholars today. All are agreed that the post-resurrection faith of the original disciples is at least the seed from which the more fully developed creed has grown.

But behind this conclusion lies the more devastating query: was the post-resurrection faith of the disciples itself securely founded, or had they got it all wrong? Granted that, after what they recognised as his resurrection, they changed their mind about Jesus, were they right in so doing, or should they have maintained their former unassured attitude? Was

167

their faith founded upon facts or, looking back under the new impulse, did they entirely misinterpret their experience of Jesus? Did a break in the continuity of history occur just here, so that, the disciples having at this point gone wrong, all the future thought of the Church was built on a mistake?

This is the agonising question that afflicts many of the rising generation today. It is the really important question of our time. Because of the doubts it engenders in their minds, many preachers and lecturers deliberately abstain from making the gospel narrative the quarry for their teaching: they prefer to confine themselves to the *kerygma*, the post-resurrection preaching. In the realms of idealistic thought they would escape from the uncertainties and ambiguities of unscientific history.

It is true that they would still affirm that theirs is a historical religion. Do they not still accept as historical fact the birth and death of Jesus and his role as teacher? But the brute fact is that the Jesus in whom they thus believe is a different Jesus from the one portrayed in the post-resurrection faith of the disciples.[6] With such a break in the continuity it is not easy to sustain the claim to be upholding a historical religion.

Their difficulty is all the greater because the gospels, from which is mainly derived the Jesus story, are themselves already written from the angle of the post-resurrection faith. The effort to disentangle from them an original unbiassed portrait of Jesus forms, as we have seen, a task of the greatest difficulty. It has resulted in the development of the most elaborate and precise instruments for the analysis and appraisal of historical documents ever conceived. It has failed in this instance to achieve the expected end, not only because the scholars engaged have not been able to agree on their detailed conclusions but also because the result expected was simply not there. As we have seen, a totally unbiassed portrait of Jesus does not exist. The authors had made up their mind about Jesus before they began to write about him. And that is true even of the originators of the oral and written traditions that were incorporated in our gospels.

In any case the gospels are honest enough about the development of belief. So far are they from suggesting that the people of Palestine recognised the truth about Jesus from the outset that they actually record the change of understanding that came with the resurrection. The disciples now recognised him as the Messiah so long promised by the prophets—but with a difference, no longer the nationalist deliverer, the royal saviour of his country, the *David redivivus*, but the 'Suffering Servant' who by his self-sacrifice rescued his people from the spiritual consequences of their failure and set them on the path of a new and more vital existence. The author of the fourth gospel says in effect, "I will tell you who this Jesus was: he was from all eternity the Word, or reason, of God who entered our world of space and time by clothing himself in the individual human nature which we came to know as the Prophet of Nazareth."

The continuity between the two, Jesus and the Christ, as we recall, Käsemann affirms can be established from four points emphasised in both the gospel narrative and the *kerygma*: Jesus' message of the love of God, his independent criticism of the law of Moses and its current interpretation, his call for obedience and love towards himself, and his death as the logical culmination of his ministry.[7] Käsemann agrees that these points afford no basis for a reconstructed biography of Jesus, but they do give to the fact of his coming certain traits of individuality. One who could stand above the law and demand for himself obedience and love was no ordinary man. If "the function of recalling the historical Jesus is thus, within the framework of the Gospel, a permanent necessity", we can without undue difficulty identify his lineaments as those of the divine Christ.

In so doing we are carrying on the biblical method of what is sometimes called 'salvation history': we are recognising the place of the divine in the material universe of space and time, we are affirming the supreme instance of God's visible entry into the course of human events.[8]

If the life of Jesus was the supreme instance of God's employment of the mechanism of history, it does not follow that his use of the method must end there. The period of Jesus was more like a watershed than an end of the road. Its immediate effect was to persuade believers that God's hand could now be even more frequently and clearly traced in human events than in the past. Acts is full of so-called supernatural events. Most characteristic is the fact that the collective wisdom of the leaders at the Jerusalem 'council' could find expression in the startling assertion "It seemed good to the Holy Spirit and to us" (Acts 15:28).

It is surprising that more in this connection is not made of the destruction of Jerusalem in A.D. 70, except in so far as it may be reflected in the apocalyptic prophecies of doom narrated in the gospels. It is probable that the Christian community was too concerned with its own divinely guided development to be unduly concerned about extraneous events. After all, in the divine providence the Christian community had become the People of God: it was what happened to them and not to the political Israel that would affect world history.

So we find that from the beginning there develops an institutional history of the Christian Church. Practically all recent scholarship affirms this fact. The days when emergent organisation was pushed into the third or even the sixth century, and the New Testament documents critically adjusted to suit that thesis, have given way to an increasing awareness of the early date of Christian institutionalism. What is called 'early Catholicism' is not now alleged to have begun with Irenaeus in the late second century but is already to be found with Matthew and Luke in the first. Acts records that the apostles are very careful to fill the vacancy in their ranks; and Paul does not fail to appoint elders in his Hellenistic churches. The creed already has its beginnings in the New Testament.[9] The sacraments are taken throughout that early period as an essential part of Christian practice; and they have already pervaded Christian thought to such an extent that some scholars have felt constrained to postulate once again the influence of pagan mystery cults in order to explain them. With such beginnings of ministry, creed and sacraments the foundations of the organisation of the Great Church were well and truly laid.

There is no need for us to tread naïvely in the footsteps of our fathers and seek some place in the great forty days between Easter and Whitsunday where detailed instructions on such matters may have been given by the risen Christ to his apostles. They follow quite simply and naturally from the life of Jesus himself and from the Palestinian environment in which he and his apostles worked. It would be possible on this ground alone to argue for Christianity as a truly historical religion. There is no evidence of any serious gap or break in the development. All that was needed was a recognition of the divine authority of Jesus, which would act as a lever and give the movement a start.

That recognition came together with the realisation that Jesus was not dead but alive. The resurrection set the seal of God upon his teaching. It was not that the Jesus of the empty tomb was different from the Jesus of the carpenter's shop. He was the same person, but now they saw him differently. They looked at him with new eyes, and when they spoke or wrote about him they used their new insight.

But if the man they had known in the flesh had not been already that kind of person they would not have been able to grasp the truth of the new understanding. As it was, the two silhouettes fitted perfectly together. They were so confident of it that they even believed that he had given them authority to carry on where he had left off. They at least were not conscious of any break between the teaching *of* Jesus and the teaching *about* Jesus. They saw the dictation of God in both with the same certainty of conviction as that with which their fathers had seen the hand of God in the safe crossing of the Red Sea and the delivery from Babylon. As then the historic events had been particular witnesses to God's abiding presence with his people, so now the human life of Jesus and the physical organisation of his Church were concrete examples of the eternal divine presence among men.

Notes

[1] Some months after this was written Miss Marghanita Laski, speaking as an atheist, made the same point in a television interview.

Conclusion

[2] Koch, *Growth of the Biblical Tradition* (Black, 1969), p. 76. Cf. also p. 130 above.

[3] Even the archival records that are believed to have come from the primitive chancellery of King David (2 Sam. 3: 2 to 5: 8) are no exception (3: 18). The easiest example is in the Book of Judges where the records of individual judges are set in a fourfold framework of apostasy, punishment, repentance, delivery.

[4] Cf. the Johannine epistles, especially 1 John 1: 1.

[5] In this connection it should be remembered that the gospels, as we have them, are Church books.

[6] This is shown by the fact that the original disciples were being led towards a belief in the divinity of Christ while the moderns are retreating from it.

[7] *New Testament Questions of Today* (S.C.M., 1969), Cf. also p. 103 above.

[8] Norman Perrin, who holds that the locus of revelation is to be found not in the ministry of the historical Jesus but in the reality of Christian experience, nevertheless agrees that there must be continuity between the two. "The Lord who spoke is the Lord who speaks" (op. cit. p. 78).

[9] Matt. 28: 19, Acts 8: 35–7, Rom. 10: 9–10, Phil. 2: 6–11, 1 Tim. 3: 16, 6: 12.

173

Index

Index